I would like to acknowledge the very generous support offered by so many people to this project. In particular I would like to thank Enterprise Foundation, Jeanette Purcell Associates and London Learning Consortium for their tremendous generosity in funding the production and distribution of this book.

Enterprise Foundation

When we set up in 1995 our founders asked themselves, 'What is the most effective and efficient way in which we can improve the long-term prospects for the UK economy?' Their answer was to assist budding entrepreneurs in establishing themselves and succeeding in a business of their own, and to set up and run successful companies that can make a positive difference in the world.

In addition to providing Enterprise Centres, we look to equip a person with the knowledge, skills and tools that enable them to grow and then maintain their business. We may also provide or source grants towards initial rent, equipment, or training. To date we have supported nearly 50 businesses to create or protect more than 1,000 jobs. In 2012 we are opening a new enterprise centre in Leeds.

We support Colin Crooks's challenge to the decision-makers in this country to focus their energies on creating 1,000 new jobs in each of the 1,000 most deprived areas of the UK.

Colin is a holistic visionary who practises, proves and demonstrates what he preaches, combining environmental and social responsibility in creative enterprise models that work. He also creates jobs, lots of them, and the people he employs are those who most need employment. In the process Colin builds a sense of community, both locally and in the wider sense of communities of interest.

George Cook
Honorary Chief Executive
Enterprise Foundation
Charity number 1048640
0300 999 2004
georgemcook@hotmail.com

Jeanette Purcell Associates

Jeanette Purcell Associates are specialists in management and leadership development. They work with individuals and businesses to help them solve business problems, manage change and develop their people.

Before founding the business Jeanette Purcell was Chief Executive of the Association of MBAs (AMBA) and still maintains a keen interest in business education. She works with several business schools and professional associations, helping them to deliver relevant, practical qualifications that meet the needs of business. Jeanette believes that business education must focus more on the development of leadership skills such as communication, people management and relationship-building.

She has written widely on this subject and is attracting growing support for her mission to reinvent the Masters in Business Administration (MBA) qualification.

JPA's approach to business is practical and unpretentious. It is driven by the simple intention to help people do business better. These values and objectives resonate with Colin's passion for giving people the confidence, skills and jobs they need to create a better society and a strong economy. Whether you're a business leader, a trainer or a social entrepreneur, you have to believe in the potential for people to change and succeed. That's why we wholeheartedly support this book's call for long-term solutions that focus on people and their employment.

Jeanette Purcell
Managing Director
Jeanette Purcell Associates
020 8297 1805
07946 385 178
jeanette@jeanettepurcell.com
www. jeanettepurcell.com

London Learning Consortium

London Learning Consortium (LLC) is a Community Interest Company that works for the benefit of communities and business across London. Our Consortium of over two hundred member organisations offers high-quality learning and skills programmes designed to meet the needs of our communities and the businesses and organisations that serve them.

Training: accredited and non-accredited programmes for learners, employees, job seekers and volunteers. Also workforce development programmes for employers, e.g. apprenticeships.

Recruitment: temporary and permanent employment and recruitment services.

Management services: professional end-to-end contract management services.

Investment: continued and growing investment in our membership and communities of interest.

This book chimes with our belief that despite numerous systems, complex bureaucracies and billions of pounds, it is people who make a difference. Enterprise, focus and social impact should be the real aims so that we can ensure real, tangible prosperity. Colin is right, challenging and beating worklessness and lack of skills is the main objective now.

Stephen Jeffery
Chief Executive
London Learning Consortium
Community Interest Company 06322097
020 8774 4040
londonlc@londonlc.org.uk
www.londonlc.org.uk

I would like to say thank you to all the people who sponsored
this book:

Michelle Weeks

David Brocklebank

Tony Golding

Ken Munn

Steve Johnson

Jonathan Straight

Matthew Wilkinson

Sinead McBrearty

Gail Biggerstaff

Andrew and Alison Makower

Colin Blears

Jonathan Essex

Henry Stewart

Frank and Dorothy Crooks

Katherine Ford

Susan Monk

Karen Wilkie

Malcolm George

John and Ann Smalley

Stuart Hearn

Rachel Mclean

Claire Harcup

Paul Boothroyd

Kate Downer

How to Make a Million Jobs

To Jane
Best of luck with
Blue Patch

Cheers

Colin

How to Make a Million Jobs

A Charter for Social Enterprise

Colin Crooks

Tree Shepherd
CAN Mezzanine
49–51 East Road
London N1 6AH

A CIP catalogue record for this book is available from the British Library.

ISBN 978-0-9573530-0-8

10 9 8 7 6 5 4 3 2 1

Typeset by Martin Worthington

Printed in Great Britain by Clays

FSC
www.fsc.org
MIX
Paper from
responsible sources
FSC® C018072

To all the extraordinary social entrepreneurs who dedicate
their lives to making the world a better place

Contents

WORKING AGE POPULATION (16-64)

Economically active
30,939,000

Employed
28,343,000

Unemployed
2,625,000

JSA claimants
1,590,000

In full-time work
21,244,000

In part-time work
7,989,000

Part-time workers wanting full-time job
1,418,000

40,190,000

Economically inactive
9,250,000

Want a job
2,339,000

Don't want a job
6,912,000

WORKLESS

WANT A JOB
Or more work
6,383,000

Unemployed (seeking work & available to start work) 2,625,000	Want a job but not seeking work 2,339,000	Part-time and need more hours 1,418,000

Sick (short & long-term) 812,000	Looking after family/ home 615,000	Other reasons 439,000	Students 530,000

13,295,000

DON'T WANT A JOB
6,912,000

Looking after family/home
1,713,000

Sick (short & long-term)
1,512,000

Retired
1,415,000

Student
1,773,000

Other reasons
523,000

Prologue

When I turned sixteen, it seemed the most natural thing in the world to look for a job. There was no culture in my family of higher education and even though I had done well in my O levels, I left school.

My first job was in a stove-enamelling factory where I prepared products to be painted. This entailed long hours rubbing down fibreglass panels with emery paper to make them super-smooth. It was ghastly work and very poorly paid but I loved it. It felt as if my journey to manhood had really started and I loved the sense of independence and of being able to pay my own way.

At 23, I entered university as a mature student. This really opened my eyes to the possibilities in life and after I graduated I started to cast around for something that I could do that would 'make a difference', to use that now slightly hackneyed phrase. After several years of struggling to find a job where I felt comfortable and where I could get a sense of achievement, I started up my own waste-paper recycling business in my spare time. It was a revelatory experience. At last, I had found a way to express my social and environmental concerns and at the same time earn my crust. I already knew that I wanted to do something for the environment – something practical and real – and I knew that I also wanted to help people who had not had the advantages that I had had.

Within a few months, I had built up my business to the point where I simply had to leave my other job. That meant handing back the company car and saying goodbye to a steady income but that did not matter one jot – I felt liberated. At that time, in 1989, the term 'social entrepreneur' did not exist, but looking back, that is what I had become.

Very soon, I was operating from a small office in Brixton and employing people to drive the vans and to collect the paper. I turned to the local Job Centre as the best place to find people for the sort of work I was offering. And so began my eye-opening experience in employing people who were really struggling with their daily lives and who had very poor education and few obvious skills.

Then in November 1993, disaster struck. The market price for recovered paper collapsed overnight and I was in deep trouble. I tried to keep trading for a few months, I cut costs where I could and tried to increase throughput but it was no use – the losses kept mounting. In the end, I sold the business to a larger waste-paper company. I will never forget the day that I had to tell the staff they were redundant. They were completely stunned; they knew things were tight but they simply had not grasped how tough it had become.

Life, of course, went on and gradually I dusted myself down and started new ventures. One of my projects was based on a training scheme teaching young people to repair and re-sell white goods. The best part of this scheme was the enthusiasm that I saw in every one of the trainees. They were all young men who had been on the dole for a long time. Many said that they had lost count of the number of jobs that they had applied for. They were all so pleased to be learning something useful, a skill that they (and others) could readily appreciate. One guy said to me that he felt much more confident: 'For the first time in my life I can go to the pub and look people in the eye.'

By 1998, the experience I had had working in social enterprise made me think about becoming a local councillor. I stood that year for Knights Hill ward in south Lambeth and was duly elected (with an 18.4% swing!). I learned a tremendous amount about how local government operates and how it can make a real difference to people's lives when it works well but how it can also make them miserable when it does not function properly.

Now, as I reflect on an eventful and very rewarding 20 years or so, I realise that I have gathered a lot of experience, not just in the recycling business, but also in job creation. Throughout my business career, I have provided work for some of the most disenfranchised and deprived people in our country and I have done that in areas where the rates of worklessness are absolutely shocking. In this book, I have tried to pull all this experience together and bring to life some of what I have learnt. In doing so, I hope not only to overcome some of the prejudice that exists against the long-term unemployed but also to win support for a radically new way of helping them. Governments have attempted so many initiatives in this area but none has been based on a real understanding of what is needed in order to break the depressing cycle of unemployment, low skill and low levels of confidence. That cycle can be broken, but only if we change the way in which we look at the issue. Instead of focusing almost exclusively on top-down solutions, we need to trust the people on the ground. We need to give them the tools to work with and patiently support them as they grow an economy in their community.

This book has been difficult to write – I have struggled sometimes to settle at my desk for the hours required. My preferred mode is to do things: to negotiate, to employ people, to make things happen. But it has given me the opportunity to think beyond the day-to-day challenges of operating a social enterprise and to consider the systemic issues that constrain patient employment and job creation.

Whenever I had a moment of doubt about writing or was blocked by a period of inertia, I drew inspiration from the memory of the marvellous people with whom I have worked. The thrill and reward of helping people to help themselves was worth all the difficulties that I encountered on the way. As I write, I can already feel the pull of a new enterprise starting to tug at me – one that I hope can blend what I have learnt so far in running social enterprises with the ideas that writing this book has allowed me to develop.

If this book starts a debate about worklessness and how destructive it can be, or if others are inspired to set up their own social enterprise, then I will know that writing it was time well spent.

Introduction

At the point of writing this book, nearly 6.5 million people are unemployed or under-employed in this country.[1] In addition, a further 7 million people are not looking for work.[2] That equates to nearly one working-age person in three being unemployed or 'economically inactive'[3] in the UK.

To me this is a staggering and scandalous figure. It represents millions of wasted and stunted lives; it represents a tower of frustration, anger and disappointment. It also represents sheer, unforgivable waste. Despite this, reports on worklessness are relatively rare in the mainstream media and there is no proper discussion of the issue. Worklessness and its causes go to the heart of so many of the social problems that we face today, from poverty to immigration, from obesity to crime rates, and yet it rarely features in our national discourse. The media regularly carry stories on the prevailing unemployment rate and focus especially on the figures for youth unemployment. However, hardly anyone seems to appreciate the degree of adult

---

1 Of the 6.5 million current under-employed, 2.625 million people were unemployed; 2.339 million people (530,000 of whom were students) were defined as economically inactive but wanting paid work; and 1.418 million were working part-time but wanted full-time jobs (ONS data, May 2012).

2 These people are NOT looking for work possibly due to very long-term sickness or disability or have retired early.

3 Registered unemployed people are considered to be 'economically active' as they are looking for work.

worklessness that prevails in this country. It is as if the issue is like the bottom four-fifths of an iceberg, hidden from view. We adopt an 'out of sight, out of mind' attitude to the colossal rates of worklessness that afflict many of our poorest areas.

We ignore the issue because a very large proportion of workless people are concentrated in very deprived, isolated areas. The poverty of our inner cities and towns is frightening and getting worse. It seems to be an intractable problem with no solution. Since the Brixton and Toxteth riots of 1981, governments of various hues have thrown huge resources at these areas, and while some of their efforts have worked, most seem to have had depressingly little long-term impact. Areas that were suffering in 1981 are very likely still to be depressed now. Despite all the investment over 25 or so years, many of these communities remain at the bottom of the deprivation table. Of the 614 postcode sectors[4] with the highest levels of unemployment in 1985, 400 of them are still experiencing worse unemployment rates than anywhere else in the country. Of the remaining 214, only eight communities have seen their unemployment rate rise *up to the national average*. Eight out of 614 achieving just average levels of unemployment in 25 years?[5]

Even more extraordinary is that for many communities nothing has changed in relative terms for 70 years or more. The Special Areas (Development and Improvement) Act of 1934 defined 251

---

4 There are 9,500 postcode sectors in the UK. A postcode sector is the area denoted by the first number of the second part of the postcode, e.g. SE24 '0'.

5 A. Fenton and R. Tunstall (2010), 'Twenty five years and three recessions, how much difference have they made to claimant rates in high-unemployment neighbourhoods?', University of Cambridge and Centre for Analysis of Social Exclusion, Seminar Paper, London School of Economics. And there is little evidence that this persistence is caused by people who get jobs leaving the area and being replaced by workless people moving into an area. In 2011 a DWP report entitled 'Understanding the worklessness dynamics and characteristics of deprived areas' by Helen Barnes, Elisabeth Garratt, David McLennan and Michael Noble looked at precisely this question, analysing worklessness data over the period 2004 to 2007, and found that the 'transition' of people who got jobs and then moved away from the area applied to a very small proportion indeed.

'Depressed Areas'. By 2005, only 49 of those 251 communities had achieved a rate of unemployment better than the national average at any time in the intervening 70-plus years.[6] The proportion of people who are unemployed or workless in these areas in relation to other areas has barely changed.

Why is this issue so important? As E. F. Schumacher says, 'If a man has no chance of obtaining work he is in a desperate position, not simply because he lacks an income but because he lacks the nourishing and enlivening factor of disciplined work which nothing can replace.'[7] For too long we seem to have counted only the economic aspects of work – whether the wage packet makes someone materially better off and improves their and their children's life-chances, chances that are, of course, also defined only in monetary terms.

Unemployment is a tragedy for the individuals concerned because unemployment and poorly paid, insecure, casual employment are the root causes not only of poverty but also of a raft of other dreadful challenges such as ill-health, criminality, poor environments and low educational achievements. In her new book *Work, Worklessness and the Political Economy of Health*,[8] Clare Bambra is very clear 'that work and worklessness are central to our health and wellbeing and are the underlying determinants of health inequalities. The material and psychosocial conditions in which we work have immense consequences for our physical and mental wellbeing, as well as for the distribution of population health. Recessions, job-loss, insecurity and unemployment also have important ramifications for the health and wellbeing of individuals, families and communities. Chronic illness is itself a significant cause of worklessness and low pay.'

6 A. Fenton and R. Tunstall (2010), 'Twenty five years and three recessions, how much difference have they made to claimant rates in high-unemployment neighbourhoods?', University of Cambridge and Centre for Analysis of Social Exclusion, Seminar Paper, London School of Economics.

7 *Small is Beautiful - A study of economics as if people mattered*, by E. F. Schumacher, p. 54.

8 Clare Bambra, Professor of Public Health Policy, Wolfson Research Institute for Health and Wellbeing, Durham University.

Worklessness also has a very negative effect on the wider society. Its steady increase has huge ramifications for our society and these became all too obvious during the riots of August 2011. However, the problems caused by worklessness go far deeper than the outburst of lawlessness that we saw then: it has a chronically corrosive and degrading effect on our society and our feelings of security and well-being. We have intensely discussed and debated the reasons for and the effects of the 2011 riots, but we have not examined or properly analysed the more insidious and destructive chronic problems that were the cause of those terrible events.

For too long we have focused on the symptoms of poverty – poor health and poor living conditions, the lack of affordable housing, and so on. I think that we should focus more on the causes. For me, worklessness is at the root of most of our social ills. I believe that helping the 15% (or one person in six!) of people who are unemployed or under-employed to get consistent work will boost their life chances and change their whole outlook.[9] Employment cannot of itself fix the structural housing problems that we see in many estates and it cannot completely overcome some of the severe accumulated health issues that afflict poorer areas. But employ-ment can increase a person's income, thereby making housing and the other essentials of life more affordable. It creates a stronger sense of self-esteem and purpose that does improve most people's health and well-being. Crime rates for an area fall if more people are in work, and if work becomes more than a remote possibility for the majority in that area. Furthermore, the increased level of self-esteem can bring with it a more pronounced feeling for the community in which one lives, and that in turn lowers the toler-ance of petty crime and vandalism.

---

9 I need at this point to say that I take a very broad definition of employment. For many it will be paid employment but for many others it will be volunteering and helping with a local community organisation or social enterprise. The key thing is the sense of purpose, the sense of engagement with society, the sense of being part of something. This doesn't necessarily involve payment, but of course that is a very desirable outcome.

I have run a number of businesses that have deliberately sought to take on people who are termed 'difficult to employ', such as the long-term unemployed or ex-prisoners. You will meet a few of them in this book. Most come to their interview, or their first day of work, with very low self-esteem and no confidence. They are often bewildered and clearly struggle with the pace of activity and the variety of things that are happening in a workplace. They are not particularly useful in the first few days either, and they make many mistakes. However, if you have the patience to wait, you will see an amazing transformation happen in just a few days. Gradually, their heads are held a bit higher, their speed of reaction increases, their clarity of speech improves. Within a short period, you can see a visible difference in demeanour. In a word, their confidence grows.

The change does not stop there, though – that is just where it starts. All our human relationships would improve if as a society we were more confident. With greater levels of confidence, you start to see more engagement with the work in hand and often with the wider work environment. Confident people start to volunteer for training and learn new skills. Confident people ask for pay rises and promotions. This in turn breeds confidence in the company, and the atmosphere of the whole workplace improves.

A lack of self-esteem and confidence is one of the root causes of obesity. It is also at the root of much social breakdown and violent behaviour. The inability or unwillingness to assert oneself when faced by an institution (whether it is the health service, the housing association, or the local council) is often an issue of confidence.

My belief is that although there is agreement in government about the statistics, and the issues they raise are priorities for all political parties, the solutions offered are divorced from real experience. Conservative and Labour governments have each in their own way attempted to deal with the staggering inequalities that disfigure our society and that seem to widen with every year. Consequently, governments have spent billions with very laudable aims but they have not achieved anything like the effects that so many anticipated. My solution is different; it draws on 22 years' raw experience of creating real jobs and helping deprived and de-motivated people from run-down communities as distinct as Brixton, Thamesmead, Gateshead, Newham, Wembley and Paisley.

This book is an attempt to look beneath the skin of some of the major issues that cause worklessness in our poorest communities, and to give life and substance to them. I will introduce you to real people who have experienced these issues first-hand and I will show you what that means in terms of their lives. I will also show what it means to employ them. In describing these people and their lives, I hope to help those who have no experience of such deprivation to empathise and to understand the scale of the challenges that prevent these people escaping from the depression of their situation.

At the core of this book is the philosophy that such ingrained challenges require concerted, long-term and patient solutions that focus on people and on *creating* work for them. Many areas of the UK have been in decline for decades and are extremely depressed. These communities are less cohesive and less resilient; they lack the skills that the modern world demands and they have a low capacity for organising. In many, a culture of dependence has formed a seemingly solid crust around the community that has restricted and hobbled all the regenerative efforts tried thus far. Turning these areas around will require patient investment and focused rebuilding. The main emphasis of this effort should be on creating new jobs in these communities. The creation of real employment is the best way to create a climate whereby new skills are valued and social cohesion is improved.

Despite the apparently bleak prognosis, it is the premise of this book that the seeds of change and hope lie dormant *within* these communities. I will seek to demonstrate that with some skill, a lot of patience and a belief in a community and its potential, it is possible to allow those seeds to germinate and to bring great improvements and energy to their landscape. It is not simply a question of *how much we invest*. It is more a question of *who we invest in* and *how long for*.

Part 1

The Unemployment Problem

Chapter 1

The scale of the problem

Unemployment and under-employment

Throughout 2010 and into the first half of 2011, some 6 million people in the UK were under-employed, i.e. they wanted work or were seeking full-time work instead of part-time. This number is growing steadily as we progress through 2012. As at May 2012, it stands at 6.38 million. Under-employment has not been this high since 1993, when it last peaked. However, throughout the period from 1993 to 2008/09 that saw steady, uninterrupted economic growth, the level of under-employment remained extremely high. Data collected by the Joseph Rowntree Foundation[10] shows clearly

---

10 From *Monitoring poverty and social exclusion 2011* by Hannah Aldridge, Anushree Parekh, Tom MacInnes and Peter Kenway, published in 2011 by the Joseph Rowntree Foundation. Reproduced by permission of the Joseph Rowntree Foundation. The chart shows the number of people who are unemployed, those aged 16 and over and ILO unemployed (wanting, actively seeking and immediately available for work), those aged 16 to 64 and economically inactive but want-

that those who are unemployed and also under-employed in the UK
has *exceeded 4 million* in virtually every year since 1992. This is an
extraordinarily high figure and it represents an unbelievable number
of blighted lives and unfulfilled dreams.

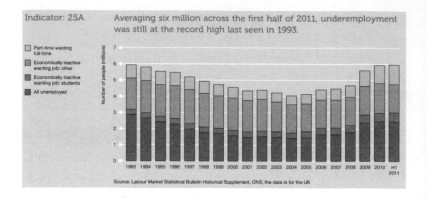

Indicator: 25A — Averaging six million across the first half of 2011, underemployment was still at the record high last seen in 1993.

Source: Labour Market Statistical Bulletin Historical Supplement, ONS; the data is for the UK

Of the 6 million people under-employed in 2011, 2.5 million were
unemployed; 2.3 million (550,000 of whom were students) were
defined as economically inactive but wanting paid work; and 1.2
million were working part-time but wanted full-time jobs. Since
then, we have seen **384,000** non-students joining the ranks of those
wanting to work or wanting more hours. The chart below, also from
the JRF report, shows the breakdown of the 'other' category within
the group of people who are economically inactive and wanting a
job, but not actively looking or immediately available to start work
(and excluding students).

ing work (but not actively seeking work or available for work – showing the split
between students and others) and those working part-time but wanting a full-time
job. Data in Charts 25A (above) and 25B (below) is for the UK.

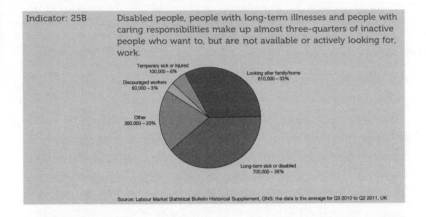

Indicator: 25B   Disabled people, people with long-term illnesses and people with caring responsibilities make up almost three-quarters of inactive people who want to, but are not available or actively looking for, work.

Temporary sick or injured
100,000 – 6%

Discouraged workers
60,000 – 3%

Other
350,000 – 20%

Looking after family/home
610,000 – 33%

Long-term sick or disabled
700,000 – 38%

Source: Labour Market Statistical Bulletin Historical Supplement, ONS; the data is the average for Q3 2010 to Q2 2011, UK

Compared with the low point in 2004, both unemployment and the number of economically inactive students wanting work is up by around two-thirds. The number working part-time who want full-time work has *doubled*. And it continues to rise – in May 2012 there were 1.4 million people looking for more hours. The huge rise in people working part-time instead of full-time indicates that the issue is the lack of jobs, not an unwillingness to look for work. Policies that focus solely on changing incentives to find work via benefit reform cannot solve this problem.

Outwardly, the most pressing problem is the high level of unemployment among young people, which is currently around three times higher than that for the rest of the population. A closer examination reveals a potentially even more damaging problem. The number of people out of work, but actively seeking work, for more than one year has rocketed in the last year. In May 2011, 11.6% of job seekers had been unemployed for more than 12 months. By April 2012, this statistic had almost doubled, to 22.3%. The vast majority of these people are over 25 years old. People aged between 25 and 49 are twice as likely as young people to be unemployed for more than a year.[11]

---

11 May 2012 ONS data: the total percentage of JSA claimants unemployed for more than 12 months was 11.6%. The 'Over 12 months' JSA claimant rate for 18–24-year-olds was 13.5%, for 25–49-year-olds it was 27.9% and for 50+ it was 32.1%!

500 QUEUE FOR JUST 20 JOBS... AT POUNDLAND
(London *Metro* headline, 18.10.2011)

This headline tells its own story: a very significant proportion of the 6.5 million want to work. The headline writers were more interested in the chance of a cheap, ironic shot at the employer.

The article revealed the fact that '*even*' graduates were in the queue for these minimum-wage jobs in Walsall. I know from experience, however, that most of the people in the queue will have been very low-skilled people desperate to earn some money and get a measure of independence back into their lives. They would have regarded these as being the sort of jobs, with the sort of skills requirements, they could do. The low level of expectation should be salutary to all of us. However, the plain fact is that many of the applicants would have been ill-equipped to do even these jobs. These headlines are repeated across the country as more and more low-skilled people chase fewer and fewer supposedly unskilled jobs as the economy moves away from this sort of basic employment. I say 'supposedly unskilled' because even in these jobs the skill requirement has grown substantially over the last few decades. Literacy and numeracy are essential (even with the use of calculators) to enable people to understand instructions, and carry out the work. Beyond those essentials, employers are looking for problem-solving skills, adaptability and a sense of enquiry. For even quite basic jobs, employers are also looking for good customer service and communication skills. More and more employers realise that in many cases their lowest-paid employees are the first people their customers meet. As firms have to fight for every customer and work hard to retain their loyalty, so the demand for a workforce with skills, and in particular what I shall call social employability skills, increases.

Later on we will see another powerful example of a retailer recruiting for new jobs – the Westfield shopping centre in Stratford – and we will see stark evidence of the paucity of skills that most of the applicants for those jobs had.

The geography of deprivation

What makes these figures much harder to deal with is that the unemployed and under-employed are concentrated in particular areas. The poverty and the lack of self-respect that goes with unemployment therefore permeates through such an area and depresses it further in the most insidious way. Again, I will illustrate this to some extent in later parts of this book. For now, let us look at the hard data on how our country is divided. The numbers are shocking in themselves but when we colour in the lives of people who live inside those statistics it can be genuinely depressing.

The graph below from work by Alex Fenton and Rebecca Tunstall[12] shows that unemployment in the poorest areas of England and Wales is persistently much greater than in wealthier areas of the country. This applies through both recessions and periods of growth. Where the average benefit claimant rate per area of the country was around 8% in 1985, the claimant rate in a depressed area could be as high as 28%. Similarly, in 2005, at the end of a long period of steady economic growth, the average claimant rate was 2% while that of the worst areas was four times worse at around 8%.

---

12 A. Fenton and R. Tunstall, 'Twenty five years and three recessions, how much difference have they made to claimant rates in high-unemployment neighbourhoods?' (2010), University of Cambridge and Centre for Analysis of Social Exclusion, Seminar Paper, London School of Economics. See also R. Tunstall and A. Fenton (2009), *Communities in Recession: the impact on deprived neighbourhoods*, published by Joseph Rowntree Foundation.

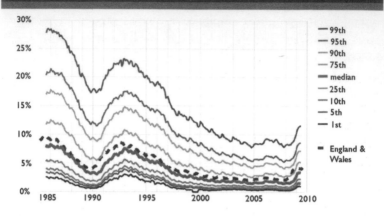

Neighbourhood claimant rates 1985-2009, selected percentiles

In addition to neighbourhood data on employment and income, the government measures the following elements of deprivation through the Index of Multiple Deprivation (IMD): health and disability, education, skills and training, barriers to housing and services, living environment and crime levels.

This is not a book about, or even inspired by, the riots in some English cities in August 2011, but it is useful to look at some of the data from the arrest records following those disturbances as a useful way of measuring why the issue of deprivation is such a concern to us all.

The figures show us that of the people arrested during the riots:

- three times the national average were unemployed;

- 50% were under 21 (which of course means that 50% were *over* 21!);

- 10% had five or more GCSE grades A* to C against a national average of 53%;

- 30% were persistent absentees from school against a national average of 4%;

- 36% had been suspended from school at least once in the preceding year against a national average of 5.6%; and

- 42% were eligible for free school meals against a national average of 12%.[13]

The Index of Multiple Deprivation records the prevalence of the major factors that have a direct negative impact on a person's well-being and life chances. The prevalence of these factors determines the nature of the whole community, and if they are too common, they will conspire to create an atmosphere of mistrust and remoteness that further corrodes social cohesion and capital.

The fundamental objective of this book is to point to an approach that will directly and positively impact on four of these seven criteria (income, employment, education and skills, and the living environment) and in so doing will help to reduce the pervasiveness of the other three (health, housing and crime). My belief is that as people gain employment or volunteer in community organisations, learn new skills and bring more money in to their household, they will gain the confidence to challenge the health system and the housing office and develop the ambition to change their way of life. I believe that empowered and confident people are less likely to resort to crime and are more likely to oppose crime when they see it happen. Most importantly they will become very strong, positive, role models for their children and other young people around them.

---

13 'How the riot statistics stack up' by Aidan Radnedge, *Metro* newspaper, 25 October 2011.

Chapter 2

What is going wrong?

As I have travelled along this road, I have drawn inspiration from E. F. Schumacher's book *Small is Beautiful*. He says, and I agree, 'It is quite wrong to assume that poor people are generally unwilling to change; but the proposed change must stand in *some organic relationship* to what they are doing already.' He describes the enormous skills deficit that developing countries experience when very high-tech plant is installed in their country. He asserts that the local community simply does not have the necessary **education, organisation or discipline** that such a technically sophisticated investment requires. In effect, it is not culturally prepared for the very different way of working that modern technology requires for its successful operation and it does not have the skills either. The problem is familiar – since the skills do not exist locally to maintain the plant, it can only be kept running by expensive, Western-trained engineers and other experts. Once the maintenance contract expires and the engineers are no longer available, it wears out and falls apart.

Schumacher's analysis of the problems faced by developing nations trying to catch up with the developed world resonates strongly to my mind with the issues that face deprived communities in our inner cities. An obvious example is the development of the Canary Wharf financial centre in the middle of the extremely deprived neighbourhood of Tower Hamlets. The shiny buildings look fabulous, they generate enormous amounts of cash and revenue, and quite a lot of that does percolate into the local area. They have even, after a slow start (and a lot of effort from the local authority, the London Dockland Development Corporation and Canary Wharf itself), seen the number of local people employed there rise to several thousand.

My point though is not to decry or debate the development itself but to illustrate the comparable nature of our inner cities to areas in the developing world where highly complex infrastructure is installed. The community already living near Canary Wharf clearly did not have the capabilities needed to take the highly skilled jobs that are the driving force of the Wharf. The development cannot be described as being in 'some organic relationship to what they are doing already'. Very few of the original residents are in well-paid jobs; most of those who do work are employed in the service sector – jobs like catering, retail, cleaning, and so on. Even more telling is that the people who are the hardest to employ are still, in the main, unemployed. The 1,000 or so people (in what is rather bizarrely termed a 'super output area' or SOA) who live just north of Canary Wharf were extremely deprived in the 1980s when the Wharf was started, and in 2007 they still constituted the most deprived SOA in London, and the 221st most deprived SOA in England (out of 32,482). The challenges faced by such inner city areas are very daunting and even the injection of large numbers of reasonably accessible low-skilled jobs cannot change the life chances for many of the people who live there. A different approach is required, something more tailored, more patient and more entrepreneurial.

Looking at the data for educational achievement in the UK we see that a frightening number of people have consistently been leaving school without elementary skills in literacy and numeracy. In the mid-1990s around 50% of children were leaving primary schools unable to read or do maths to a basic standard.[14] I suspect that this has always been the case, but that it did not show up as a problem because the economy in past years created a large number of unskilled jobs that did not particularly require those skills. As the industries that generated such jobs have steadily disappeared, the issue of basic and essential key skills has started to become more apparent. However, we have not registered the fact that an extraordinary number of people in our society are functionally illiterate and unable to do basic arithmetic. We seem to take it for granted that the vast majority of people in our society do have those skills. My experience from 20-plus years on the front line of employing people in very deprived communities has disabused me of that comforting thought and the research that I have done for this book has substantially backed up that experience. For example, more than 4 out of 10 (over 40%) of working-age people living in the most deprived areas have either no qualifications or level 1 or below (qualifications below GCSE grades A* to C), compared to only 12% of those living in the least deprived areas.[15]

Many people in these communities have disorganised and unstructured lifestyles which are simply not conducive to normal employment patterns. There are many causes for such disorganised, unstructured lives. One huge factor, for instance, is drug abuse. The Department

14 Department for Education National Curriculum Assessments Key Stage 2 in England 2010/11 (revised), published 15 December 2011. The 1995 percentage achieving level 4 or above in English was 49%; by 2011 this had increased to 82%. The 1995 percentage achieving level 4 or above in Maths was 45%; by 2011 this had increased to 80%. This means that despite substantial improvements, by 2011 one in five of primary school childrens had not achieved level 4 maths and English.

15 J. Hills et al (2010), *An Anatomy of Economic Inequality in the UK*, Report of the National Equality Panel. Data quoted is for England, Highest Qualification, Labour Force Survey 2006–2008 by Index of Multiple Deprivation deciles. 'Working age' is defined in this instance as women aged 16 to 59 and men aged 16 to 64.

The Unemployment Problem

of Work and Pensions estimates that over 360,000 people who are claiming some sort of out-of-work benefit are serious drug addicts. Drug addiction is far from being the only cause of individuals leading chaotic lives; depression, mental illness, family breakdown and many other factors all play significant roles. Typically, the most deprived areas have fewer community organisations to represent their interests. This shortfall in capacity further restrains their ability to organise coherent plans for the types of development they want.

For me Schumacher's third key word, 'discipline', should nowadays be read as 'work culture'. By work culture, I do *not* mean knowledge and skills; I mean a basic understanding of what work is and what behaviours are expected and necessary when you go to work. Work culture includes things like turning up on time, taking instructions, speaking clearly, looking at people when they are talking, booking time off, adhering to break times; yes, the absolute basics. I have worked in many areas with high rates of worklessness. In such areas, it is almost normal not to have work and a large proportion of what I term 'social employability capital'[16] has been lost or seriously eroded. I have met and employed a large number of people who just do not understand or value the ideas of attendance, reliability, applying themselves at work, learning new skills and gaining experience and knowledge. They simply do not understand the concept of progression through experience and application, and they feel that the rewards are too small and the delay too long. It seems so easy to trade some drugs or pass off some stolen 'gear'; these rewards are quicker to arrive, and larger too.

We need to offer a new and better example of how to win real respect and build relationships based on steady employment, learning new skills and broadening horizons. The challenge is very big but I believe that we can create the conditions that will help many of these deprived and marginalised people to find and hold down jobs and learn new skills that will transform their lives.

---

16 'Social employability capital' describes societies' understanding of what work is and what behaviours are expected at work.

Chapter 3

A deepening crisis

The problem of long-term unemployment has been with us for a very long time. In the eighties and nineties we heard the expression 'underclass' used to describe this tier of our society that seemed unreachable and was in all practical terms beyond the pale. Commentators reflected on the fact that we were losing the sorts of unskilled jobs that typically occupied people with really low skills levels.

That underclass did not go away, despite the apparent boom years of the mid-nineties to 2008. The number of people defined as suffering from worklessness remained stubbornly at 4–5 million throughout that period. No matter that we have spent billions on huge regeneration projects and that business was booming across almost all sectors.

For several years now there have been a very significant and daunting number of people for whom work is either a distant aspiration or an impossible dream. This fact alone should loudly proclaim to all policy makers, of whatever political persuasion, that their standard solutions (whether they be more capital and infrastructure investment, or more interventions on the supply side such as streamlining planning or liberating housing markets) will not have any impact on that huge number of unemployed citizens.

The UK has lost an enormous number of jobs in manufacturing and we are consistently being urged to move into areas of ever higher technology to stay ahead of the low wage costs competition. This means that the nature of even the lowest-paid modern work is becoming more demanding: it needs an ever higher level of the social employability skills that I referred to previously, as well as literacy and numeracy skills; it requires very high levels of personal organisation and communication skills. As consumers demand ever better levels of service and as products are increasingly customised to meet specific customer needs, each job acquires more aspects and a more acute need for clear and empathetic communication as well as accuracy and reporting. As businesses become more intricate, more technologically driven and more focused on customer service so skill levels and, above all, the prevailing *attitude* to work will become increasingly large factors for businesses deciding where to locate their operations.

In drawing up a business plan for locating a business, the proponents will look at a wide range of factors such as the cost of the property, the proximity to their market and the availability of raw materials and logistical access. They will also take a close interest in the skills available locally and see whether they match the skills requirement for the business. Any investor looking to bring business and jobs into an area of low skills (perhaps because the property rents are lower) will need to reflect carefully on whether they will be able to find sufficient people with the skills that they need in the locality. The educational, social employability and personal organisation skills deficit commonly found in areas of deprivation means that it is increasingly difficult to attract business to such areas.

The fact that people with low or no skills are significantly more likely to be unemployed and to live in areas of multiple deprivation will not come as much of a surprise, but I think the scale of the differences between areas will shock many readers. There is a vicious circle formed of worklessness, low skill, low self-esteem and the area in which people live. Each aspect compounds the effects of the other. A critical mass of individual difficulties and issues often build up to create a cultural landscape in which work and enterprise are unfamiliar, even alien concepts.

In order to enable us to help the individual, we have to create a new community dynamic. We need to galvanise and energise the latent creativity that is often dormant or suppressed in deprived communities. By doing this and releasing that energy we can change the atmosphere and the spirit of a place and get people working together. In their report on immigration and social cohesion in the UK, the Joseph Rowntree Foundation (JRF) made the following observation that supports this view: 'The researchers conclude that to ensure cohesion, the impact of social and economic changes needs to be addressed *as well as* how people relate to each other [my italics]. The limited opportunities and multiple deprivations of the long-term settled population in parts of UK towns and cities undermine social cohesion. These fundamental issues of deprivation, disadvantage and discrimination impact on both majority ethnic and minority ethnic settled residents.'[17]

I believe that although these challenges are daunting, we can address them. There are solutions to these problems: we can rebuild communities and peoples' lives and we can restore hope.

---

17 Joseph Rowntree Foundation Report, 'Immigration and social cohesion in the UK', Mary Hickman, Helen Crowley and Nick Mai, 20 July 2008.

Chapter 4

The importance of adult employment

We need to look at the unemployment picture as a whole: it affects people of all ages, in all areas of the country. However, as Julia Unwin, Chief Executive of the Joseph Rowntree Foundation, said on BBC Radio 4's *Today* programme on 1 December 2011, 'the most effective way to address poverty is to create jobs for the long-term unemployed'.

It is, of course, vital that we do something to ameliorate the unemployment of young people; we know that being unemployed in the early years of adulthood severely and permanently blights a person's life chances. We also know it will reduce their lifelong earning potential and their employability. They are our future, as is so often said, and we should invest in that future by working very hard to create jobs for them.

However, the long-term unemployed are the most disadvantaged of all. They are the ones who have already suffered exactly the same fate as we anticipate for the young unemployed now. Not only are they very disadvantaged financially and have few resources to cope with any of life's shocks, but they also make very poor role models for younger people trying to get work. If we can create work for those older people, we will address three issues simultaneously:

- we will create new positive role models for others (including the young unemployed) who live near them;

- we will start to tackle their ingrained poverty and lack of engagement with society; and

- we will start to make reparation for the lack of effort we put into their education and the terrible impact that had on their life chances when they were young.

Parental role models

A major theme of this book is the powerful effect of role models, both positive and negative. People respond to the examples set by other people and in particular those set by their parents or other responsible adults.

The impact of parents on their children's learning achievement is well understood. A substantial body of large-scale research exists into the relationship between various parental factors (such as social class, educational achievement and working career) and the school outcomes of children. There is a considerable level of agreement between these studies that factors beyond the school gates are more material than the schooling itself. Indeed, in a recent interview for the BBC's *Analysis* programme broadcast on 30 January 2012, a leading authority in this field[18] stated very clearly,

after you adjust for the achievements of children when they start school, there are further effects related to their social

---

18 Professor of Social Statistics Harvey Goldstein, from the Centre for Multilevel Modelling at the University of Bristol.

The Unemployment Problem

background, whether they are a boy or girl, their ethnic background. These background factors, social class, income, etc., have very important effects very early on in childhood and, of course, these persist throughout schooling... The school effect tends to be rather small; once you have taken account of all those factors maybe it accounts for 10% of what's left – which is not enormous.

It turns out that the biggest single factor that determines a child's educational outcome is how well that child's parents did at school. In other words, the life experiences of the parent are far more important determining factors than the choice of school when it comes to a child's education.

However, the projected outcome of a child's education is not set in stone by what happened to its parents at school. Indeed even quite late in a child's education – in their teenage years – it is possible to set them on a path towards achieving above their expected educational attainment. An intense and complex study by the Institute for Fiscal Studies[19] calculated that of all the factors that would explain a child's performance in secondary school, less than half relate to that child's experience during primary school.

Their report says,

> What can we conclude from these results? While the notion that 'skills beget skills' suggests that it remains important to invest as early as possible in a child's life in order to reap the greatest benefits of later investments, the fact that only 40% of the gap in attainment at age 16 can be explained by what has happened up to the end of primary school suggests that, even during secondary schooling, it is not too late to intervene to try to close the socio-economic gap. And while our results certainly cannot be regarded as causal, it is

19 Institute of Fiscal Studies (2011) Working Paper 10/5: 'The Role of Attitudes and Behaviours in Explaining Socio-economic Differences in Attainment at Age 16'.

interesting to note that a sizeable proportion of the gap in progress between ages 11 and 16 seems to be explained by our observed measures of parental and child attitudes and behaviours.

It is my contention that working sets a powerful, positive role model for children. This is especially so if the parent is employed in an environment which encourages learning and training. The encouragement to study, engendered through the parent's parallel training journey at work, is a very strong counter-balance to that same parent's low achievement record at school.

However, working is not only a significant role-modelling behaviour in terms of learning. Research from New Zealand[20] suggests that where a parent or carer earns a living through employment it seems to boost confidence in the children and enables them to achieve more than where the parents receive benefits:

> Research on the source of income consistently shows that welfare income is negatively associated with children's outcomes. Most (but not all) studies also show that even after controlling for total family income, welfare receipt is still negatively associated with children's outcomes.

Other adults as role models

The role model effect continues to work, well beyond formal schooling. In chapter 17 we will see several examples of how young adults, without any background in learning, can be switched on to engage with formal instruction. It is equally important, though, that young people acquire the social employability skills that are critical to finding a job in the modern employment market. In this regard, role modelling is the only effective method of instruction.

---

20 'The Influence of Parental Income on Children's Outcomes' by Susan E. Mayer, Knowledge Management Group, Ministry of Social Development, 2002.

Take my friend Bert. You will read much more about him later, and indeed you will hardly credit that the Bert I first met is the same man that I will describe now. Bert was in his mid-fifties when I met him; he lived on an estate near Brixton and he was married with two children. He and his family absolutely personified the work ethic. At various times they were all employed by me and they were all great workers. They were also fantastic role models. Everyone who came inside their orbit – and it was a large orbit – seemed to catch the work bug.

Early in 1993 my recycling business, Papercycle, expanded into a much larger space along Coldharbour Lane (in retrospect this was not my greatest business decision!) where we took over a huge paper baler that could make 500kg bales of waste paper or cardboard in minutes. I had no hesitation in asking Bert to be my foreman. He had been a consistent, hard-working and reliable driver for me and had readily organised the other drivers as the business had grown. Moving into such a large space and actually doing the baling of the paper ourselves meant we needed more people. Quite a few came to us via the Job Centre, but Bert also brought in quite a few waifs and strays that had gravitated to him or his family. Most of them did not seem very good prospects when they first arrived, but Bert had a knack of getting the best out of them and persuading them to engage with the jobs at hand. They all *wanted* to work but most of them frankly didn't really know where to start.

We had taken on a young lad called Keith, and over time, he had proved himself a good worker. I will tell you more about him later too. For now though, I'll tell you the story of his brother.

One day Keith turned up a bit late with a grey-looking young man who he introduced to us as his brother Jake, who'd just come out of prison. (Keith had met him at the prison gate, so that's why he was late.) I didn't need to be told the prison bit: Jake had that prison-induced pallor that I had come to recognise. We needed an extra hand so we took Jake on for a trial. At first, he was very hard to work with – surly, unresponsive and slow. I warned Bert that I could only give him a week or so to shape up or he would have to go. Well within the week I could see a change, and after a couple of months he became the supervisor when Bert was away. He had completely blossomed into a hard-working, very well-organised supervisor, but I have to say I would not have credited that as an outcome on day one!

There were many more people like Keith and Jake who Bert brought in and helped to turn around. Not all made it, I will admit – some could not cope with the physical nature of the work – but most of them did.

Perhaps the greatest surprise was a man called Geoff. I had met Geoff several times at Bert's house and he'd struck me as the classic hanger-on – there was always food, tea and a warm radiator at Bert's, and Geoff could regularly be seen there enjoying all three. Geoff was not able to work at Papercycle as he was not fit enough to lift heavy weights, but a year or so after Papercycle had closed Bert asked me if I could help him set up a new business. I was very pleased to be asked and when I came to talk through the business and how it would work, there was Geoff at the forefront with Bert. He worked really hard on getting that business going and it was obvious to me that something of Bert's zeal had rubbed off on him.

Positive adult role models have a direct and significant beneficial effect on other people. Parents are clearly the biggest influence in a child's early years development and they continue to have a major influence on a person's level of ambition, their willingness to engage with learning and their confidence about their future. It is never too late to invest in a person and that investment often has a multiplier benefit. In training an adult you not only improve that person's skills but you also create a role model for their children and other adults and young people.

The Unemployment Problem

Ralph's story

Ralph came to see me in June 2011; he explained that for the past five years he had been a 'house husband' (a local euphemism for being unemployed) and had virtually given up on getting a job. He thought no one would give him a chance and that nobody valued him as a person. He offered to work for nothing, to volunteer – he'd do anything – but was clearly agitated and didn't know what he could offer. As we spoke it became obvious that not being at work was affecting his family and in particular his relationship with his young son. What sort of example was he being?

We talked, and after a while, he said that he used to ride BMX bikes and enjoyed fixing them. I took a punt. We accepted him on our volunteering programme with the understanding that, if he stuck at it, after three months I would seek funding for him to get a qualification in cycle mechanics.

He did stick at it, and we did secure the funding for him through Sustrans to go on a course at BikeWorks which would lead to a City & Guilds level 1 qualification.

In December 2011 were able to secure a contract with the local council to provide a cycle re-cycle scheme. This has enabled us to employ Ralph and an additional staff member on paid 18-hour contracts.

Ralph has changed since he started with us. He's proud of working for us, his son comes in to help and he even shows his wife around the workshop. The introverted Ralph who we first met in June has gone – he now happily talks to visitors about his work, and how much he enjoys it. Recently our premises were broken into. When we phoned him to let him know, even though it was his day off, he came round within two hours to check his workshop.

Ralph is a great role model and you can see that he inspires the volunteers he works with. He supervises two younger adults and they look up to him and want to please. He is a typical man's man, and also gets on well with the younger volunteers.

We gave Ralph an opportunity, and he's paid us back many times over. The change he has made to his and his family's life is great; the change he is now making in other people's lives is an unexpected bonus.

(*This story was related to me by the General Manager of a respected charity in eastern England.*)

Financial resilience

Saving for a rainy day is something that all sensible people try to do. We put a bit of cash aside for those times when we need it really badly – in illness, unemployment, or having to travel to help a sick relative. Moreover, saving is what parents do to support their children and help them get on and make progress.

Bert was able to pay for his son's HGV driving lessons after Phil lost his job on a building site. He had worked incredibly hard to put that money away and had made many sacrifices along the way. But salt it away he had, and the positive effect on the whole family was tremendous when Phil passed his HGV test and went on to get a job as a truck driver.

For so many families, though, such savings are all but impossible. The analysis carried out by the National Equality Panel in their 2010 report entitled 'An Anatomy of Economic Inequality in the UK'[21] compares very starkly the resources[22] available to the

---

21 J. Hills et al (2010), 'An Anatomy of Economic Inequality in the UK', Report of the National Equality Panel.

22 Drawing on data from the Office for National Statistics (2009), 'Wealth in Great Britain: Main Results from the Wealth and Assets Survey 2006/08'.

The Unemployment Problem

least deprived people in our country with those available to the most deprived. After taking into consideration all the savings and money held in cash or in current accounts and any debts owed, the survey shows that 25% of the population effectively has no financial assets whatsoever.

Household financial wealth 1: summary statistics, 2006–08
Great Britain, whole population

	Mean	1st quartile*	Median	3rd quartile
Gross financial wealth	43,500	800	7,200	37,700
Net financial wealth	40,000	0	5,200	35,200

* lowest 25% of all households

There is an enormous gulf between those households with property in the least deprived areas and those in socially rented property in the most deprived areas. Those in the richest areas have a median average wealth 14 times greater than those who live in the least well-off areas.

Making reparation

Aside from the pragmatic reasons (making positive role models and relieving poverty) for creating employment for unemployed adults with low skill levels, there seems to me to be a moral imperative. We will see in chapter 9 that literally millions of people were let down by the education system in the decades following the Second World War. The system failed to recognise that work was changing and that the skills required to succeed in work were changing too. It seemed acceptable that children coming from poorer backgrounds should receive a lower standard of education. As a result, many people were left totally ill-equipped to deal with rapidly changing circumstances and have struggled all their lives to provide for themselves and for their families. Now, as we face what looks like a very long recession for some areas[23] they are ignored again.

The media and the politicians alike focus on the terrible problem of youth unemployment, but seem to pay scant attention to adult unemployment, which is a far greater problem both in sheer scale (61% of unemployed people are over 25)[24] and in impact on society, because most of the adult unemployed are parents as well. Their children will suffer from the poverty that unemployment brings and their educational outcomes are being negatively impacted as well.

Is it fair to ignore such people twice? They were ignored at school and now they seem to be written off as almost impossible to employ because they have so few skills. Is it their fault that the system failed them so badly when they were children?

We need a policy that focuses most energy on those that need most help to get into work – irrespective of age. The social benefits of such a policy would be substantial and I believe it would also be the most effective long-term method of stemming the flow of unskilled young people into our jobs market.

---

23 Although statistically the nation will emerge, no doubt, from recession it seems certain that this will be because specific sectors of the economy, such as finance, will do above averagely well and that other sectors will continue to decline. For those other sectors there will be a continuing recession.

24 Office for National Statistics, Labour Market Statistics May 2012, ILO unemployed January to March 2012 in the UK, Labour Force Survey.

Chapter 5

My proposal

There is a clear, causal link between the terrifying scale of unemployment and worklessness that exists in certain areas of our country and a raft of other social ills that afflict those who are unemployed, and indeed permeate through the whole of society.

This presents a very clear challenge to policy makers and business leaders. How can we create real jobs for the millions who have been unemployed (or under-employed) for a long time in areas that are conditioned to high levels of unemployment?

In search of the answer, I was inspired by the book *The man who planted trees* by Jean Giono. In it the narrator describes how before the First World War he went hiking in the area where the Alps merge with Provence. After three days of walking in a 'barren and colourless land' he describes finding himself without water in the 'midst of unparalleled desolation'. He finds a small hamlet but it is completely deserted. Quite by chance, just as he starts to lose hope, the narrator meets a shepherd, Elzéard Bouffier, who takes him in and gives him shelter. Over the next few days, the narrator watches Elzéard as he patiently selects and then plants hundreds of acorns right across the valley. Day in and day out, he plants the acorns with his trusted dog as his only company.

Ten years or so later, after experiencing the horrors of the First World War, the narrator returns to find a lush wooded valley where clean streams bubble through the landscape. The acorns and other seeds that Elzéard Bouffier planted are now young trees. The branches of the young trees are providing shelter for new plants and their roots are holding in moisture. The narrator sees people setting up home and building schools.

It is an enigmatic, apocryphal story but it sums up the philosophy of this book and I hope will serve as an effective metaphor for the combination of a trust in (human) nature, long-term commitment, focused application and patient investment that I am advocating. For me the acorns are the individuals who live in the area who have an idea for making it better. The hard, seemingly infertile soil in which Elzéard planted his acorns is analogous to the harsh world of our inner cities where talent does not flourish and where (legal) enterprise struggles to succeed. Typically, but not exclusively, in such an area the people will be unskilled, poorly educated, relatively unhealthy and on or close to living on benefits.

However, I believe each of these people has real potential and spirit. Over the last 22 years, working across inner-city London and with others in other inner cities, I have seen that when that spirit and that potential is reawakened, amazing things can happen. I have seen what I call the redemptive power of engaged employment and I have seen what is required to create that engagement. I have also seen and experienced some of the issues that in my view prevent the creation of engaged employment and what prevents a business community from settling and establishing itself.

Just as Elzéard Bouffier committed years of his life to steadily planting individual acorns to create a lush forest, we need to begin a patient, dedicated and concerted effort over many years to rebuild our most fragile and blighted communities. The effort needs to concentrate on revealing and developing the skills, organisation and confidence of the people who live in that community. We should then provide intense and concerted support for, and investment in, the local people and organisations that are motivated to create businesses in these deprived areas specifically to relieve the scourge of unemployment and worklessness. Simultaneously, we should support the local people and organisations that are dedicated to helping their community to address the wider range of social and environmental issues that afflict it.

If we carry through this work in a patient and dogged way we will get to a tipping point where quite suddenly attitudes will change, both outside the area and, more importantly, inside it. External investors will be attracted to the area. The proximity to the city centre and major urban markets is an attraction, as well as relatively cheap space, and those factors, combined with an engaged and reasonably skilled workforce within walking distance of the workplace, will make the location a very compelling proposition.

Part 2

Barriers to Employment

Chapter 6

The skills shortage

A major problem facing many of the unemployed in the UK is their lack of skills. In this chapter, 'skills' should be understood in their broadest sense. I shall introduce you to several people whose lack of basic skills such as literacy and numeracy caused them real difficulties, both at work and in the outside world, and to several others who simply had no idea of what work entailed or what it could offer.

The quote from a government report below sums up the dilemma facing those who are trying to help such people to find work:

> One employment manager from Knowsley said, 'We get lots of clients saying "I just want to be a labourer on a building site; I need my CSCS card."[25] But again, the way things are going now, just to be a labourer on a building site you still need an NVQ2.' Another manager, in Bradford, observed that male clients often express an interest in plumbing or gas fitting without possessing the basic skills required to access the vocational courses. These statements reflect the findings

25 Construction Skills Certification Scheme.

in other research into the growing difficulties the long tail of unskilled workers face in competing for a declining number of unskilled jobs.[26]

Low skill levels – an employer's eye view

I have employed many people with very low levels of skills over the last 20 or so years. The following stories are intended to illustrate the challenges that employing them can present.

One of the biggest concerns is the terrifying levels of functional illiteracy and innumeracy.

Weighing up the problem

In the early nineties, jobs in Brixton were at a premium – especially low-skilled ones. I would post one relatively low-paid labouring job with the Job Centre and within hours I would have a queue round the depot.

It would be a very mixed bag of applicants. Some were clearly working the system and attending a compulsory interview; some were almost completely incoherent; but many were, to be frank, desperate. After another round of exhausting interviews I had found a young man called Billy who, although incredibly inarticulate, had something about him, and I'd taken him on to work on the paper sorting line.

Billy did indeed have something about him and very soon he was operating our brand new drink cans sorting machine, which could separate aluminium from steel cans and then crush and bale them. It could process four tonnes a day, which is a lot of cans (roughly 200,000). At a business level, this was a fantastic machine and a real step up for us, but operating it could be a very dirty job as the drips and spillage from the cans seemed to go everywhere. Billy excelled at it and also proved to be very good at dealing with the customers who

---

26 From the New Deal for Communities evaluation report.

came in to sell their cans to us. He would run their cans through the machine, the steel ones would be plucked out by the magnet and the aluminium ones would shoot through into a basket, which was accurately weighed, and we would pay on that weight.

One day I had asked him to weigh in about 40 bags of cans that a customer had dropped off early that morning. I wanted to get a feel of how many steel cans there were in a typical mix and to do that I needed the weight of the bags before he processed them. It was not a very sophisticated operation – it involved a set of fish scales! I needed him to list the weights of each bag and bring me the list. After about half an hour, he came up with the list. I looked at it and was totally bemused: he had roughly written down two columns of numbers that read something like:

Bag
1. 2.5 – 5
2. 3.0 – 6½
3. 2 – 4½
4. 1 – 2¼
5. 2.5 – 5½

I said, 'Billy, what does this mean?'

He replied, 'It's the weights you wanted.'

'But why so many numbers?' I asked.

'That's what it says on the scale things.'

'Show me?'

Down he went and came back with the fish scales. Then I realised what he meant. He'd been reading across both scales: kgs and lbs! When I explained these were two different scales, he said, 'Nobody told me!'

This lack of numeracy (and the almost inevitable attendant illiteracy) meant Billy got into lots of difficulties. Once he told me he was about to be evicted. I asked why and he didn't really know. ('I dunno' was his most used expression.) When I phoned the landlord (which was a housing association), they explained that Billy was in arrears but what had brought the situation to a head was the fact that he had not responded to any letters. When I explained that I was his boss and that if possible, I would be happy to deduct his rent from his wages and pay the housing association directly plus a small extra amount to repay the arrears, the matter was resolved. Billy stayed in his house and I continued to benefit from a very reliable worker.

Dyslexic stress

I have often been told, 'You don't need to be able to read very well to be a driver.' Really? Let me tell you the story of Gavin.

Gavin joined Papercycle as our first full-time driver. He was a young man who was very affable and obviously intelligent. His parents were very wealthy but for some reason that we only came to appreciate later he did not have a great relationship with his family. He really wanted to drive a van and earn his own money, so after several conversations with the insurance company he hit the road. He got on very well. Early feedback was that he was completing all his scheduled work and that the customers loved him.

Then after he had been about a week on the job, we came back from lunch to a tirade of answering machine messages from Gavin, each call getting more and more desperate and abusive. 'Where is this ****ing place, I can't find it!' and 'Why have you sent me here – where the **** is it?', and so on. We could not work out what the problem was and we could not contact him (no one had mobile phones then) so we had to wait for him to come back, which he duly did, somewhat late and very subdued and angry.

'Where the **** is Richmond Road?' he asked.

'That's the Bridgman Art Library,' I said. 'It's in Hackney.'

'I know that,' said Gavin, 'but where is it on the bloody map?' Together we opened the A–Z, found Richmond Road E8, and looked up the page and the map reference.

I said, 'There it is.'

'Where? – I can't see it.'

'There, in that square,' I said.

'I still can't see it, can I?' said Gavin.

Well, Richmond Road is quite a long road and in our A–Z the road name is printed R I C H M O N D   R O A D in a very spaced-out way spread across the width of the page. Gavin, it turned out, was dyslexic and just could not cope with words that were so spread out, and that curved with the road. He just could not read it. Now at last we had started to realise what was at the heart of his problem with his family, why they hadn't backed him to go to university and why he was here with us driving a van. His dyslexia had completely held him back and made him virtually a pariah in his high-achieving family. It was also holding him back in a really basic job. Worse than that, many employers would have sacked him after listening to the tirade of abuse we got down the answerphone! The story had a reasonably good outcome. We paid for Gavin to go on a programme to deal with his dyslexia and he eventually left us for a much better job.

Mapping the problem

Gavin's not being able to read very well led to a moderately entertaining story and no real harm was done. Well, it didn't turn out that way with Victor.

He came to us for a trial as a van driver. He interviewed well and came over as confident and competent. I met him by the van the following morning and for the first five jobs, I read the map while he drove so I could check his driving. I only had one van and I needed to know that he could drive it properly. On the sixth job just outside Paddington station, we got back in the cab and I told Victor that

I would like him to read the map from here. He refused. He said I should read the map as I was here. I said I normally wouldn't be with him and that he would be on his own, so I needed to see that he could find his way around. He stubbornly refused to take the A–Z and I equally insisted that this was an integral part of the job.

Then suddenly he hit me. Just out of the blue – 'smack' in the head – twice. In the cramped space of a van cab, we started grappling with each other – him enraged and me stunned and bewildered. Eventually, Victor calmed down and we sat there panting and staring out of the window. My head ached and my ear hurt, but fortunately, there was no blood.

After a while, I asked Victor, 'Can you read?'

'Naw,' he mumbled.

I said, 'Well, let's finish the round the way we started and I'll pay you for the day and we'll call it quits.'

So that's what happened. He drove and I read the map. We collected all the paper and came home. Needless to say Victor did not pass his trial. I paid him for the day's work and I never saw him again.

I learned something that day. Never put someone in a position where he has to admit he cannot read. He will have spent years carefully honing and developing tricks to avoid the question and if he is caught out, he may well have to resort to violence because he just cannot admit he cannot read.

Illiteracy at work

After Gavin and Victor, we started to test all potential drivers on map reading at the interview. What an eye-opener that was. Out of 52 people I subsequently interviewed for the driving jobs a full dozen (yes, nearly ¼ of the applicants!) could not read. One held the A–Z upside down, another even started on page 1 and ran his finger along every road, hoping he might just *find* the right one. Three others just walked out of the interview. It was painful to watch but it was at least a relatively safe way of finding out if they could read.

That was in the early 1990s and things have clearly not improved very much, as the extract from the *London Evening Standard* of 1 September 2011 below shows:

SCANDAL OF LONDON'S ILLITERATE JOB-SEEKERS

On the bright side, the flood of applications for jobs in the new Westfield Stratford shopping centre shows that the development has brought much-needed employment opportunities for a formerly depressed part of London. There are about 20 applicants for each position. But the fact that Westfield has had to provide literacy and numeracy training because many of the new employees cannot actually fill in application forms and some have difficulty adding up is more sobering. For those brought up here, it is an indictment of the education that they have received in at least 11 years of full-time schooling.

This paper's literacy campaign, Get London Reading, has identified the extraordinary numbers of children in London with poor reading skills – about one in three 11-year-old boys, for instance, has the reading age of a younger child. The campaign has also identified the contributory causes of illiteracy – the number of pupils who speak English as a second language, for instance, in areas of high immigration and the number who move between schools. But what is also obvious is that there are schools that are far more successful than others, even in similarly deprived areas, in teaching pupils to read. Some schools simply perform badly. And of course there are teenagers who lack any will to learn and parents who fail to help them.

It is to the credit of Westfield that it is prepared, with the help of a government-funded agency, to remedy the schools' and families' failings. This is not unique; other companies and institutions such as Tesco and the armed services have also had to teach recruits basic literacy and numeracy. But they should not need to do so. If schools are not equipping their pupils with basic skills, they are failing at the most fundamental level and some heads and some teachers should be sacked. There is probably no more urgent priority for government than to ensure schools equip young people to enter the workplace.

Hundreds of staff at the huge new Olympic shopping mall had to be taught to read and write after bosses found they could not even fill in basic forms.

Employees at Westfield Stratford City have been given remedial tuition after Australian director John Burton made the "incredible" discovery that they were illiterate.

The boss of the £1.45-billion mall said he was amazed that so many have left British schools without basic skills. He told the Evening Standard: "The most difficult thing was the number who simply do not meet the basic reading and writing criteria.

"They could not even fill out the forms without getting assistance. They just weren't ready to interview."

His discovery is the starkest example yet of the literacy crisis in the capital's deprived areas which inspired the Standard to launch its Get London Reading campaign aimed at training adults to provide literacy support to primary schools in poorer areas.

The remedial education blitz comes as Newham council said it is set to exceed its target of securing 2,000 jobs for local long-term unemployed at what will be Europe's largest urban shopping centre when it opens on September 13 next to Stratford's Olympic Park.

But Mr Burton, who has lived in London for seven years, said the most dramatic discovery was how many applicants for work on the site had been failed by the education system. He added: "We brought tutors in for the people we thought might make it because their enthusiasm levels were high.

"Some of them were here for many, many weeks so that we could identify where help was needed and correct those defi-

-ciencies. As an Australian I found it incredible people here can side-step all the checks there are in school and still fail the basic tests when they are the age for employment."

Low skills impede promotion

At the GreenWorks depot in Woolwich, an area notorious for its high levels of multiple deprivation, we needed a new manager. In line with our policy of developing our own people, we decided to promote our existing supervisor. He had made quite a good impression at that level and had organised the day-to-day logistics for three vehicles reasonably well. I knew there was an issue with written reporting but we convinced ourselves that we could overcome it. Peter was keen at first to take on new tasks, and for a while, we thought that the appointment would work out. As time progressed, however, and the true gulf between the manager's job and Peter's actual skills level became more and more obvious, we started to realise that we had a problem.

The first issue was getting anything in writing from him, such as a weekly report on the depot covering such things as jobs completed, revenue earned, staff issues, costs incurred, etc. Then it became obvious that Peter was really uncomfortable with the numbers involved in the job. We had been vaguely aware of both of these issues and we were prepared to work with Peter on them.

The real challenge came when, over the period of a few weeks, it became apparent that he wasn't able to organise and manage the extra complexities of the management job and lacked the confidence to actually manage. Where he'd had clear daily instructions as a supervisor he was comfortable and reasonably competent, but when asked to take on the manager's role himself it was a step too far. At the heart of the issue was a lack of education that really prevented him from understanding the business beyond a superficial level. His inability to plan or to manage a project much beyond the next day meant we were in crisis-management mode almost all the time.

We certainly learned some hard lessons from this episode – about being more careful who you promote of course, but also about the huge level of investment and effort that would be required to raise someone's skills level when their educational foundation is very poor.

Applying our newfound wisdom

A while after our experience with Peter we decided, again in accordance with our ideal of developing our staff, to promote a driver to the role of supervisor. She had excelled as a driver and was clearly the most responsible of all the crew. She knew the ropes and understood the essential nature of preparedness and planning. She was also a very clear communicator (sometimes a bit too graphic!) and got things done. However, while she had a lot of natural talent it was equally obvious that her numeracy was not very strong and her supervisory and reporting skills were underdeveloped.

From the start, we adopted a weekly meeting and review process that set out in quite a structured way all the issues that she would have to think about: the staff, the vans, planned maintenance, health and safety, staff leave, the customers, and so on. Very quickly, she grasped the ideas at the heart of this process and was very soon ahead of herself and the weekly meeting. We would talk on the phone about issues before they really became problems. Her ability to plan forward grew rapidly as she learned from the process of reporting what had happened previously and where things had not gone to plan. By learning through experience and, more to the point, recording and discussing the experience she developed into a very effective supervisor.

The shortage of management skills

The lack of higher-level skills in terms of numeracy and literacy meant that we regularly struggled to find local people who could fill a supervisory or management role.

My management style is fairly typical and it will sound very familiar to many readers – 'Bring me solutions, not problems.' By this, I mean that I would expect a manager or indeed a lower-level supervisor to be able to see a problem, work out what he or she thought was the cause and articulate a solution. My role would be to look at the proposed solution, test it, challenge it, and if it passed muster to give it approval. If it required investment, I would need to give the manager the authority to spend the money.

Instead, what we consistently found was that managers were not able to assess the problem in the first place. They knew there was a problem but did not have the skills to work out what was causing it, let alone to come up with a solution or put a cost to that solution. Relatively straightforward exercises had to be done by senior management or myself: exercises such as managing delivery rounds, making sure the vehicles were used efficiently, ensuring that customers were not let down by internal overbooking, measuring which products (desks or chairs) sold the most, measuring which day was the busiest in terms of furniture coming in or of customers coming to buy. At a fundamental level this was due, I feel, to a lack of higher-level skills such as the ability to analyse data, develop spreadsheets or write structured reports. Consequently, staff had not really trained themselves to step back, capture data and make informed decisions with good data at hand.

These sorts of problem-solving skills are not taught easily in a training course or a classroom; they are learned through experience and action and honed over time. It is especially difficult to teach these skills on the job in a small business, because the supervisor or local manager is often the only senior person on site and the whole site is very dependent on their judgement.

From an employer's point of view this lack of skills is very debilitating. It adds costs right through the business from initial recruitment, through training and supervision, to customer service and quality monitoring. It also puts a significant premium on these key skills that pushes up the overall cost of labour.

Beyond the financial cost, there is also a human cost. There is the obvious stress and strain that such underperformance puts on all the other members of staff; but there is an untold story of the stress it puts on the individual who is not up to the job through a lack of skills and education. That individual becomes further disillusioned and demotivated and each time they lose a job their confidence falls further. It does not take very long at all for the sense of disillusionment to be overpowering and dominant to the point that a person can give up trying.

Chapter 7

Other difficulties at work

Unreliable quality

People who do not understand the basic concept of work have no realisation of how important it is to be on time, or to phone in if they are sick or if they have had an accident.

We employed one 22-year-old, Angus, who was an excellent worker. He started with us on a New Deal[27] programme and while he was on the programme, he was very reliable and solid. He was bright and keen to learn, so at the end of his time with us we offered him a job as a team leader. He was a natural; he understood what needed doing and could get his team to work very hard. He was intelligent and had an easy charm that meant he was very good with customers and colleagues alike.

Unfortunately, after a couple of weeks of promising performance, he started to become very unreliable. At first, he would

---

27 New Deal was a major employment support programme introduced in 1998.

turn up late but soon he was missing whole days. What made matters worse was that he never called in and he never explained. We told him repeatedly that timekeeping was essential, especially as he was responsible for a team now. Moreover, we explained that his employment contract was equally clear about calling in if he was sick. After many episodes, we started a formal process of warnings and went through our discipline procedure. After every instance, we asked him to explain his absence and every time he said it would not happen again. However, within days, he would arrive late once more. His team started to fall behind in its work and that had a negative effect on the other teams. It started to create unrest in the warehouse and we knew we had to do something, as he was setting a very poor example.

We tried to understand what was causing his poor attendance and to find out if he had any particular issues at home. After a while, we concluded that he was an alcoholic. While we were more than willing to work with him and to help him, we were not equipped or trained to help someone suffering from this illness. In the end, he could not change his behaviour and we had to dismiss him. This was a very sad end as he had so much potential.

The story highlights how important social employability skills are to employers. If the employee is unreliable, it is impossible to give him any responsibility and it is difficult to justify any investment in his or her training. The story also highlights that employing people who lack these key skills is very demanding for the employer, and very difficult to achieve. For me, though, it also suggests that any strategy of job creation for long-term unemployed people needs to contain some sort of support or mentoring that can help people overcome the difficulties such as alcoholism that prevent them from holding down a job. When you consider the tremendous potential of people like Angus, it would prove to be a good investment.

Low-skilled work – the view from the ground

It is the view and perception of those who are long-term unemployed or who are in fragile or uncertain employment that I want to share with you now. Generally, it is quite hard to find the voices of those who are in this position, so to start with let us look at low-paid work from the point of view of two senior executives who put on their overalls and went '*Back to the Floor*' (a BBC TV series).

'I think we exploit them'

Modern employment at the bottom of the ladder is a very fragile and uncertain existence. However, despite the low pay and the insecurity, these jobs demand increasingly high levels of skills both at the basic level of numeracy and literacy and at the higher communication and supervisory level.

In *Back to the Floor* Grant Whitaker, Pickford's director of UK removals, was moved by what he found when he went to work with his men in the Birmingham area. And he was honest enough to admit it. 'With some of our people, the way we employ them and the way we reward them is wrong,' he said. '*I think we exploit them, take advantage of them. They are employed on a part-time casual basis, but some of these guys work almost permanently for us, yet have no holiday or sick pay.*' (My italics.)

He went on to say, 'The whole exercise was fascinating from my point of view. It showed me how important it is for the rest of the business to support the people on the front line. They are probably the lowest paid, but they are the most important. They deliver the service. They are the vital link: the face of Pickford's. It is their interpersonal skills that matter in dealing with stressed-out customers. Each job is unique, and they have to think on their feet and can often be really quite resourceful.'

Whitaker, who returned to HQ covered in bruises but carrying a 25-point action plan, was exhausted at the end of his week. He went on: 'It is damned hard work. I was new to the job, but I believed that I understood the concept of the moving business. But, in fact, I just didn't appreciate the complexities and dynamics.'

The dynamics hit Whitaker hardest when lack of the latest equipment meant he had to hump a heavy safe down stairs or get a double wardrobe out through an upstairs window.

The complexities hit home when he discovered the movers have to find a public call box or beg to use someone's phone when they need to talk to the operations department. While Pickford's is a multi-million-pound business and its trucks travel the world, the guys on the ground had no mobile or vehicle communication system.

The most telling point of this story is that despite being fundamental to the success of the business, the removal teams have the worst employment terms and are taken for granted. Whitaker undertook to review their contracts and improve their working conditions. He also said that he would provide the crews with communications equipment that would make their work easier.

'Our men shouldn't have to deal with that'

When Tom Riall, managing director of street cleaning company Onyx, was told that his workforce's morale had hit rock bottom, he was determined to find out why. Ditching his pinstripe suit in favour of regulation binmen's boots and uniform, the 40-year-old, £90,000-a-year boss joined a £5.95-an-hour crew on the City of Westminster shift. Here Tom describes what it was like getting his hands dirty...

'As part of the management, I'd only heard complaints from customers against our dustmen, but I soon saw the other side. It incensed me how irresponsible traders and members of the public can be. A West End restaurant, for example, had made no attempt to seal leftover food properly and as a result the bin bag was crawling with maggots. Our men shouldn't have to deal with that, so I went into the restaurant and demanded to see the manager to make a complaint. The job can be very hazardous, too. Bags are packed with glass, syringes, tins of fat and paint. Just one shard of glass could cut a collector's leg open…'

This is another example of low-paid work that is physically hard, very demanding and quite unpleasant. Neither job commands a lot of respect but both require very high levels of attendance and reliability, and these requirements in turn demand a very robust constitution. It is easy to see that working in these sorts of environments would not be attractive or even possible for many people, and the nature of the work and the attendant lack of opportunities to develop could give the whole concept of work a bad reputation.

Tom returned to the office with two commitments. The first was to overhaul the overtime payments system to make sure the staff got paid properly and on time. The second was to look into why the vehicles were so unreliable.

'I'm not making the tea!'

Many long-term unemployed people do not appreciate the dynamics of the work environment. They simply have no idea that you can work yourself up from very lowly jobs.

Take the lad from a training programme who I just happened to catch leaving GreenWorks early on his first day.

'Hi,' I said. 'Where are you going – it's a bit early, isn't it?'

He replied, 'I didn't come here to make tea all day – I'm off.'

I said, 'Hold up, tell me more.'

He said, 'I've made the tea twice now and I'm just not doing it no more for no one.'

On talking to him some more I realised that this lad honestly thought that tea-making was as far as he was going at GreenWorks and that every day would be like that. He had no sense of progression because he had no sense of what was involved in work. When I explained that first days are often very tedious, but as you become known to everyone and as other new people join, the work gets better and you are given fewer of the tedious jobs, he seemed almost surprised. Anyway, he stayed on and gradually he did work his way up. In the short time he was with us, he seemed to learn a huge amount. We talked a few times and he explained how his mum and dad didn't work, how they'd both done time in prison and how he'd never had anything like a settled routine or achieved anything in his life.

I got to thinking how much of an impact upbringing has on people, both in obvious ways and in many much more subliminal but equally important ways. I remembered then how my little boy reacted to me putting on a suit for a wedding one Saturday morning. He was no more than eighteen months old and as he watched me putting a tie on he said, 'Daddy go work now?'

Even at that young age, he had noticed that 'work' was a thing that had its own routine, its own dress code. Well, I thought the opposite must also be true. If your parents have not worked all your life, you have never seen that routine. You will not have seen different clothes being prepared, never have witnessed Dad or Mum rushing to get the train or bus in the morning, then coming home happy after a good day (or returning tired and grumpy after missing a promotion!). You will never have heard the 'You'll never guess what so and so said in the office today' conversation, or 'I've got an early start in the morning'.

In short, you have no formative understanding of what 'work' is.

Do we have to wear heels?

Most low-skilled people struggle to appreciate the benefits of training because they cannot see beyond their immediate needs. At Cybercycle, we got a contract under the New Deal programme in 1998 to train young people in how to fix computers – to actually work on the hardware. As part of the arrangement, we sat in on an interview between the New Deal coordinator and two young unemployed kids in Brixton. We watched as Michelle explained that under New Deal she could get them on a Microsoft Word course where they could learn to type and word process and arrange files, and so on. The lads barely lifted their eyes off the floor but after a period of silence one said, 'That sounds like girls' work – do we have to wear high heels?' They were absolutely not interested in anything that was remotely associated with secretarial work and just would not engage.

This misperception of what work consists of, how you can develop and how different skills might become useful is a serious limiting factor when it comes to getting people (young and adult) to consider different jobs and to apply for them. While it is true that it is easier to get a job if you've got a job, it is equally true that it is easier to get your first job if you have at least a basic perception of what a job is and what it can lead to.

Learning what work entails

In the stories in this chapter, we see stark examples of the social employability gap. This gap is almost impossible for most employers to bridge. In most companies, if someone walks out on day one because he is asked to make the tea, no one will chase after him and try to persuade him to give the job another chance. If a new person is late more than once (and in some companies, they get no chances!), they'll be sacked. If a person can't see the relevance of the training they are given and doesn't want to engage with it they will struggle to make headway at work and will be the first on the list when redundancies are considered. In each of the cases described above, there was a tremendous amount of potential that could be unlocked. I have included the example of Angus to show that it is not always possible to overcome the barriers and that there is no guarantee of success. Yet the overall results that a patient, empathetic and engaged employer can achieve are amazing.

In areas of very high endemic unemployment a number of families experience what is often termed inter-generational worklessness. This term is used where two or even three generations of the same family have experienced irregular work, low pay and long periods of unemployment. It is an incredibly depressing thought, but it is a relatively common phenomenon in such areas. This is a significant factor in the loss of social employability skills that I have remarked on elsewhere. Where a family has no positive role models for work it is likely that its members will have a very poor appreciation of what work is, what happens at work and what benefits (apart from earning money!) can be gained from it in terms of self-respect and enhanced life skills. Much of the employment available in these areas is of the type described above: casual, low-paid, insecure and often dirty and physically demanding. Why would someone with an extremely limited perception of the possible benefits of work take on such low-paid, uncertain work when it will put their benefits at risk or reduce them substantially?

Large numbers of people do take on this work, which is testimony to the fact that most people value work and the self-respect they get from it and do not want to be on benefits. But it must also be the case that for those inexperienced people who have no concept of what work actually is, these jobs offer very poor examples of what work should or could be. Without any contrary examples, they will only see the one, negative side of work and very rarely get an insight into the positive side – the camaraderie and the sense of fulfilment that even the most arduous, dirty jobs can provide.

Chapter 8

Social barriers

Beyond the social employability skills that I have outlined and illustrated above, there are other very corrosive issues that inhibit a person's ability to focus on work and destroy their confidence.

The problem of debt

Debt is a major stumbling block. Take just one example of hundreds that I have witnessed.

Joe was a loud Scouser who drove for me at Papercycle. He was tall and wiry but possessed immense strength and could pick up huge bales of paper from one of our clients where everyone else needed help. He was, in short, a fabulous worker, keen, enthusiastic, high-spirited and engaging. After a few months he became quite introspective, and he started arriving for work a bit late. Then he didn't come in for a couple of days, which of course was really frustrating as I had customers to serve and collections to be made. One Thursday morning he walked in slightly late and clearly very distracted. I called him in.

'What's happening, Joe? What's wrong? You need to tell me or I can't help you – and frankly your job's on the line here, so tell me!'

After a long silence (I have discovered that the best way of getting anyone to talk is to shut up!), it all poured out. His wife had left him; she took their joint credit card and blew £4,000 on it and then promptly disappeared. The bank was on his case and they were making his life hell. He couldn't concentrate; he didn't know what to do or what to think. Should he just run away and change his address as his wife had done?

'What are they saying, Joe? Have they written to you?'

He showed me a letter – it was very threatening and intimidating and I could see why he was so scared.

'Do you mind if I call them?' I asked.

'Go ahead, Boss,' he said dejectedly.

Eventually, I got through to the appropriate manager and I explained who I was and what my interest was. I said that as his employer I would make sure he made a payment every month to the bank. We went through what he earned and how much his rent was, and so on. After about 30 minutes, the manager said, 'Well, can he afford £5 per week?'

I said I was sure he could and the deal was done there and then. Joe was ecstatic when I came off the phone. He just could not believe it. They were not going to send the bailiffs round? They would not take him to court? And yes, he could afford £5 a week.

'Thanks Boss!' he exclaimed and he bounced out of the office with such a spring in his step that he nearly cracked his head on the door-jamb.

The threat of the debt and the pressure from the bank had pressed down on this powerful man so much that it had stopped him from being himself: the person he prided himself in being – Joe the hard worker, Joe the reliable. And the removal of that issue, or at least the managing of it, brought him back to life just as surely as if I had resuscitated him. He was a new man and he worked even harder for the next few months.

I occasionally see Joe even now. He is a bus driver, he has a new woman and his life has moved on. He always refers to the moment described above when we see each other and it clearly made a big impact on him. I feel privileged to have played a part in his story at such a difficult time for him.

Coping after prison

Debt and low income has a further-reaching impact than just on the individual who is in debt.

Take Sandra, for instance. She was a serving prisoner who was with us on the Release on Temporary Licence (ROTL) programme. She was an excellent worker and was doing really well in the sales office. Initially she'd started in sales administration as she didn't have the confidence to meet real customers, but as time went by and her confidence grew Sandra started to deal directly with customers and proved a real hit with them. The prison service was supportive in this process and we as employers felt we were part of a team helping Sandra to build her confidence before she was released.

As it turned out her release on parole came at a time when we were looking for a full-time sales assistant and we offered her that job without hesitation. So one Thursday evening she left work an inmate of the prison and the following Monday she came into work as a free woman. Almost immediately, though, we noticed a change. She was often taking time off, normally without calling or asking, and she was very preoccupied. When she was at work, she was as good as ever, but her attendance became increasingly inconsistent. The prison service was unable to help us, as she was no longer in their care. The probation service did not pick up the baton and provided no support to GreenWorks whatsoever.

We talked to Sandra about her timekeeping and her absences and she was very defensive. At first, she would only tell us that she had 'a lot of things' to sort out. Having been in prison for so long, she needed to do things like re-register with a GP and find a dentist.

However, these did not justify all the absences and there were clearly other concerns that were much more complex than registering with a GP. We tried to communicate with her probation officer but he was very unhelpful and despite the fact that we were providing her with work, the one thing that the probation service considers critical to a successful rehabilitation, we could not have a meaningful dialogue with him.

Slowly, we found out that the issue of most concern was a domestic one. She had moved in with her sister, as that was the most convenient place to stay. This was not ideal as her sister lived in an area not too far away from where Sandra had become involved with crime. It also meant she faced a long and difficult journey to work. I think she would have done better to try to find somewhere to live nearer to work and further away from her old life. Her sister did not work and so from day one she treated Sandra as a 'cash cow' because she had a job. The domestic pressure was quite intense and created real difficulties for Sandra that affected her work performance. Despite all this, Sandra tried hard to improve her timekeeping because, as she said to us, 'Coming to work is keeping me away from the situations that got me in trouble before.'

In the end though, the timekeeping just got worse. After six months of trying very hard to get her back on track, even we had to give up and Sandra had to leave us. We never discovered the underlying cause of the issue but I am certain that if we had had more cooperation from the probation service and more engagement from the prison service at the point of her transition to life outside prison we could have made more of a difference. As it was, we were at least able to help Sandra find her feet in those crucial first few months after release from prison. She kept out of trouble during that time and I heard later that she had settled down and started a family.

This experience was repeated several times over. We employed a number of prisoners on release from prison and within a few weeks, their performance would decline due to external pressures around housing or from past associations. There is absolutely no support or guidance on offer to employers and there seems to be very little liaison between the prison service and the probation service. The situation is crying out for reform. I believe that we could have achieved much better results for everyone concerned – ourselves, the released prisoner and the probation service – if the services had been more coordinated and if we had been able to work as partners with the probation service. A small amount of support for both the prisoner and the employer in that crucial few weeks post-release would improve the resettlement process and reduce recidivism.

Mobility problems

Beyond the individual issues that people face there are also substantial structural problems for people on low wages trying to get work.

The Joseph Rowntree Foundation (JRF) has consistently highlighted one very significant barrier to employment for disadvantaged or low-skilled people: travelling long distances to work. One of their reports reads:

> Work-related mobility is largely confined to those with higher skill levels for whom there is a national labour market. Nationally, those in elementary and personal service occupations have the lowest median travel to work distance (less than three kilometres) while those in professional occupations have the highest (around seven kilometres).[28]

I had started to become aware of this barrier in the late 1990s when I was with Cybercycle. There we offered job search support to the trainees on our New Deal-funded computer repair facility. One young man noticed what looked like a good job. It was well suited to his experience, but it was in Walthamstow, on the other side of London. He completely dismissed it at first as impossibly far away.

---

28 'Local initiatives to help workless people find and keep paid work', Pamela Meadows, Joseph Rowntree Foundation, 26 June 2008.

To people familiar with commuting to work the idea of such a journey would not have been daunting, but to him the distance and the fare were real barriers. We eventually persuaded him to go for it but it took a lot of effort.

A while later when I was running GreenWorks I noticed that my accounts assistant, Larry, was looking really tired. We had recently taken him on full-time after he had been on a New Deal programme for several months. His skills were not great but he was keen and could do the basic books for us, and we thought we could train him to do more. He had been delighted to secure a 'proper' job at the end of the New Deal placement as he had been unemployed for two years, and as he was now in his fifties he was really worried about his future. When I asked him if he was OK, he explained that he was tired from the bus journey; I said I thought he got the train into work. He explained that when he was on New Deal his train fare was paid for by the office (the Job Centre), but now he was employed he had to buy his own ticket, so he was using the bus as it was cheaper.

'But the bus takes ages,' I said.

'Yes,' he said, 'it takes two hours each way.'[29]

So in order to save around £3–4 per day, Larry was spending an extra three hours on a bus grinding through south-east London. No wonder he was so tired. The problem was that, being on just over minimum wage, the cost of travel was a very significant factor in Larry's budget and he preferred to travel long hours to reduce those costs. Fortunately, our plan to secure a warehouse in Woolwich came to fruition quite quickly and we transferred the accounts function there, which reduced Larry's travelling time to less than 10 minutes.

---

29 The train, by comparison, covers the 10-mile journey in 37 minutes, even with a change at London Bridge.

People really want a job

As the programme at Renew (the white goods repair company) developed, we won a contract with North Tyneside council to provide training to some of their residents. The contract was a good one but we were nervous about how it would work in practice. The travel to work distance for the trainees was much longer than we had ever considered before. Some trainees would have to get three buses (their fares were covered under the training fee) to work and the start time was 8 a.m.[30] Most of the trainees were from very deprived families where there was a culture of unemployment. They would be getting up alone and leaving the house as early as 6 a.m. to come to the training programme. When you add all these things together, you start to understand the extent of the challenge.

Well, they all made it in to work on day one and yes, they all came back for day two. Within days, they had settled into a travel routine and very soon became a strong unit that worked and learned together. Not only did they work hard but also, after a diffident start, they began to take an active interest in how the project was being run and especially how their learning was being handled. Some of their feedback was uncomfortable for the trainers to hear at first, as it was bluntly expressed in words of one syllable, but it was honestly given and it did drive improvements. As an added bonus, the trainees steadily developed their diplomacy skills. In terms of future employability, this was the biggest gain because, as so many employers are constantly saying, the 'softer' communication skills are at least as important as technical skills.

So we proved that where the training makes sense and is about relevant skills, even the most deprived young people would go the extra mile to make something of it. More to the point, their sights soon rise and they can and will really engage with the training and take an active role in improving it.

---

30 We were intent on mirroring employment practices in manufacturing firms as a vital part of developing training and job preparedness.

But they also need help?

The external social issues I have illustrated above are additional to those I have already highlighted as the social employability gap. The most effective response to such issues is for the employer to work with others, such as the probation service for example, and coach the individual. In that way they can be helped to find the best solution to their problems. I do not mean completely work out a solution for them (although sometimes that is what happens) – I mean working with them and coaching them to sort out their own answer.

Clearly, this demands a lot of time. Unfortunately, time and patience are the two things most often in short supply in the average business! Moreover, time and patience needs to be mixed with empathy if the help given is to be effective and well received. I do mean empathy too, *not* sympathy. Sympathy is the last thing that these people need. They need practical help and guidance and a bit of space in which to learn from their mistakes.

Summary

At the last count there were upwards of 6.5 million people suffering from worklessness and many more in low-paid, low-skilled employment. Unfortunately, this very serious state of affairs does not receive enough attention and yet it lies at the core of most of our most intractable social problems.

Unemployment and under-employment saps people's confidence and their energy. It makes them lethargic and affects their health. The shortage of money dramatically reduces their choices in terms of where they can live, what food they can afford and how far they can travel. It leads some of them into crime.

Work is probably the best route through which to address things like the mental pressure of debt or the sorts of social pressure that can lead to criminality. A real job creates a new imperative and the incentive to get to work and to learn new skills. I am sure that if Joe had been unemployed when he received the demands from the credit card company, he would simply have run away. The long-term consequences of not dealing with the issue would not have occurred to him. Equally, Sandra could easily have been sucked back into the ways of her past if she had not had to get up early to go to work.

Unfortunately, their approach to work is conditioned by a toxic mix of negative factors. Typically, they will have poor education in the basic skills of literacy and numeracy and suffer a terrible lack of social employability skills. They will live in areas of high unemployment where attitudes to work are skewed by negative perceptions, poor experiences and a lack of opportunity.

I do *not* believe, though, that the majority of people who are afflicted by long-term unemployment are either lazy or feckless. In fact, I believe the opposite. Despite being the least well equipped in our society, many of them overcome extraordinary odds to get into work.

Such communities and individuals are stuck in a vicious negative cycle. The traditional way of framing this conundrum is 'They can't get a job because they don't have the skills; they can't learn the skills because they don't have a job.'

I would reverse the conundrum: 'They can't get the skills because they don't have a job; they can't get a job because they don't have basic or social employability skills.'

The preceding chapters cover some huge, complex and chronic problems that together make getting employment for many people an insurmountable challenge. Governments of all political complexions have attempted to tackle the issues. Tremendous resources have been expended but have had relatively little success. In the following sections, we will examine what has been done to date.

Part 3

Current Solutions

Chapter 9

Supply side initiatives

There are essentially two main approaches to relieving worklessness. The first and most commonly pursued approach is the supply side route. By this, I mean preparing individuals to get into work through re-skilling, CV preparation and interview training. The argument for the supply side approach is very sensible. The nature of employment is constantly changing and the skills required to get jobs are therefore constantly changing too. We must invest in training and education so that people can acquire the skills they need to be successful in the employment market. We must also make it easier for people to travel to where the work is and encourage a flexible housing market to enable people to move if necessary.

'We need to improve the schools then'?

'Let us reform our schools, and we shall find little reform needed in our prisons.'[31]

---

31 John Ruskin, English critic, essayist and reformer (1819–1900), *Unto This Last*, essay 2 (1862).

One of the obvious conclusions to draw from our high levels of functional illiteracy and innumeracy is that we need to improve our schools. We know that if we give children a good, well-rounded education that is strong on English and arithmetic, we will set them up for life. Education is clearly fundamental to the success of our country and our society. Consequently, it forms the biggest single supply side intervention made by the government. The current government projects that it will spend £89.5 billion in 2013, which is a massive increase in spending from the £39.1 billion spent in 1998.

However, to focus solely on investments in school improvement ignores four major concerns:

- Improving schools does not address the issue of those who have already left school with very poor results.

- A full *90%* of a child's educational outcome is determined by their domestic circumstances.

- We have a long way to go before we achieve a universal 'good' education standard.

- Improving schools is a long drawn-out process.

The legacy of our national failure to invest in education prior to around 2000 is deeply shocking. The latest data from the Labour Force Survey[32] shows that in 2012 there are an extraordinary **9.8 million** people (yes, nearly one in four of our working-age population) who do not have a single level 2 qualification (equivalent to GCSE A* to C or NVQ2). This is a staggering number, which has to be acknowledged before any meaningful strategy can be developed to increase employment. We have to accept the fact that a frightening proportion of our working population is ill-equipped for the high-tech, high-value employment upon which we appear to be pinning so much hope. We have to accept the population as it is, not as we would like it to be.

---

32 Department for Business Innovation and Skills Quarterly Statistical First Release, 29 March 2012.

The ramifications of this for our society extend further than the immediate employment prospects for these people. We have also to consider the next generations. When we remember the enormous role model effect that parents have on their children it can be no surprise that, even after we have invested billions in education, large numbers of children are leaving school with barely any qualifications.

The charts on the next few pages clearly show how far we need to improve the educational system in this country in order to provide even a basic minimum standard of attainment for all our children. They also illustrate how difficult that challenge will be and how long improvements take to happen.

Consider this first chart. It is from a JRF report[33] and it shows educational attainment (reading and arithmetic) for children aged 11 between 1995 and 2010. Level 4 is a basic reading or numeracy standard that all children leaving primary school should attain. In 1995, 50% of our children were leaving primary school unable to read to that standard and a staggering 53% could not meet the numeracy standard. It seems likely that the figures for the period before 1995 were, if anything, worse.

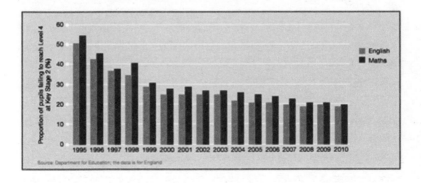

33 From 'Monitoring poverty and social exclusion 2011' by Hannah Aldridge, Anushree Parekh, Tom MacInnes and Peter Kenway, published in 2011 by the Joseph Rowntree Foundation. Reproduced by permission of the Joseph Rowntree Foundation. The data is for England.

By 2001, thankfully, we had seen a dramatic improvement in the numbers meeting this standard, but by 2011 we were still sending around *one in five* of our children to secondary school with inadequate levels of English and maths, with the figure as high as one in three of those eligible for Free School Meals (FSM).[34]

The situation is not much better at secondary school. In 2005, more than 60% of 19-year-olds in Inner London lacked a level 3 qualification (equivalent to A level), and an extraordinary 40% of 19-year-olds in Inner London lacked *any* level 2 qualifications (O levels to me; GCSEs for younger readers).

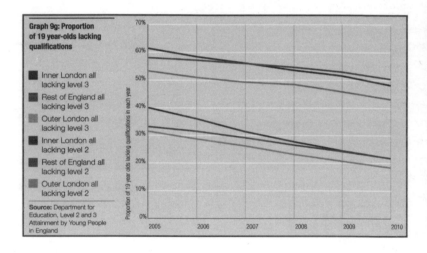

Graph 9g: Proportion of 19 year-olds lacking qualifications

- Inner London all lacking level 3
- Rest of England all lacking level 3
- Outer London all lacking level 3
- Inner London all lacking level 2
- Rest of England all lacking level 2
- Outer London all lacking level 2

Source: Department for Education, Level 2 and 3 Attainment by Young People in England

The enormous investment that went into education during the 'noughties' did produce significant results. The level 3 deficiency fell substantially in all areas of the country and the level 2 deficiency fell by

---

34 Percentage achieving level 4 or above, Key Stage 2 in Maintained Schools in England in 2011: 81% all pupils, 67% eligible for FSMs, 85% not eligible for FSM; see Table 9a, Department for Education Statistical First Release, SFR31/2011 published December 2011, http://www.education.gov.uk/rsgateway/DB/SFR/s001047/index.shtml.

nearly half everywhere.[35] These are impressive results but they also show that we are still, even after all that investment, sending a considerable number of our young people out into the world without a single GCSE.

Concentration of the poorly educated

The improvements in educational outcomes are not evenly distributed. The following map of London[36] shows the distribution of 19-year-olds lacking level 3 qualifications by borough. It is clear from the map that low educational achievement is concentrated in particular areas of London.

---

35 Though attainment of level 2 and 3 by age 19 continues to rise, by 2011 around one in six (16.2%) of 19-year-olds were still lacking level 2 or higher qualifications and 43.3% were not qualified to level 3. There is also a notable gap in attainment at age 19 between those formerly eligible for Free School Meals at academic age 15 and their peers who were not eligible for FSM. In 2011, in England, more than one-third (34.8%) of young people who were eligible for FSM at 15 had not achieved level 2 qualifications by age 19, compared to their peers where the lack of attainment was one in six (16.2%). There is also a level 3 attainment gap at 19 between young people who were previously eligible for FSM and those who were not. In 2011, more than two-thirds (68.2%) of 19-year-olds previously eligible for FSM at age 15 were lacking a level 3 qualification, compared to their peers where the figure stood at four in ten (43.5%). See Department for Education Statistical First Release, 'Level 2 and 3 Attainment by Young People in England Measured Using Matched Administrative Data: Attainment by Age 19 in 2011', published April 2012.

36 T. MacInnes et al (2011), *London's Poverty Profile 2011*, published by Trust for London and the New Policy Institute.

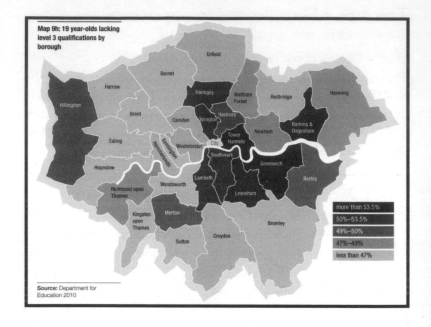

Map 9h: 19 year-olds lacking level 3 qualifications by borough

more than 53.5%
50%–53.5%
49%–50%
47%–49%
less than 47%

Source: Department for Education 2010

Education is not enough

Supply side employment strategies therefore have to contend with the fact that a substantial proportion of the adult unemployed are very poorly educated; and not only this, but they have also missed acquiring the habit of learning, or in many cases do not appreciate the benefits of learning. Therefore, whereas re-skilling does work for people who have been made redundant from a declining industrial sector and who appreciate the need for skills and training, it is unlikely to work well for those who have no such experience.

CV preparation and interview training fall into a similar difficulty. It is very hard to make a CV look good when a person has so little experience to write about, or as my mum would say, 'You can't make a silk purse from a pig's ear.'

The lack of employment opportunities

There is, however, a far greater challenge to the supply side approach. There simply are not enough jobs to go round. A recent analysis by Paul Gregg, Professor of Economic and Social Policy at the University of Bath,[37] suggests we need to create upwards of *5 million* jobs if we are to help the most deprived in our society. The table below shows how Professor Gregg breaks down the numbers:

Welfare Crisis. We need 5 million new jobs.	
2.5 million	Unemployed
1.5 million	Older workers potentially staying in work
0.8 million	Disabled people who the government is trying to bring into activity
0.2 million	Working age population increase per year plus likely continued increased participation of mothers

Add to this the rapidly increasing numbers of part-time workers (1.4 million) who really want full-time work and it is easy to see that the need for employment completely dwarfs the number of vacancies available. In May 2012, the ONS (Office for National Statistics) reported the total number of vacancies as 457,000.[38] Leaving aside the large number of applicants who already have jobs, this means that there are 14 workless people for every vacancy. What makes these numbers even more daunting is that the people behind the statistics are largely invisible to the general population. As Professor Gregg shows, drawing on analysis by the Office for National Statistics, the rates of employment have remained steady or even improved for marginalised groups

---

37 Professor Paul Gregg, University of Bath, 'What's going on in the Labour Market', presentation at the Social Market Foundation, October 2011.
38 ONS Labour Market data, May 2012.

such as lone parents, ethnic minorities and disabled people. *However, for those with the lowest educational attainment or who live in the most deprived areas they have declined markedly.*

This can be seen in the graph below which shows the employment rate for the residents of the most deprived areas has declined since 2005 from around 65% to just above 60% (implying of course that almost 40% are either unemployed or economically inactive). For those people with poor education the rate of employment has declined from 60% in the period 2003–2007 to 56% at the end of 2009.[39]

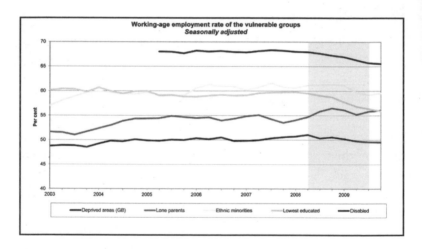

This graph shows how the employment of some marginal groups improved, i.e. lone parents, ethnic minorities and the disabled, BUT not the lowest educated or those living in the worst areas.

The analysis by the ONS also looks at employment rates by how many disadvantaged groups a person belongs to. For example, a

39 Analysis based on Labour Force Survey data for Great Britain. See P. Gregg, University of Bath, 'What's going on in the Labour Market', presentation at the Social Market Foundation, October 2011and R. Barrett, Office for National Statistics, 'Disadvantaged groups in the Labour Market', *Economic and Labour Market Review* vol. 4 no. 6, June 2010.

Current Solutions

person living in a deprived area may also have low levels of qualifications and be disabled. The ONS analysis shows a striking contrast between levels of employment and multiple disadvantage. For example, in the period October to December 2009, if an individual did not belong to one of the disadvantaged groups identified, they had an employment rate of 83%, whereas if someone belonged to three groups, the employment rate dropped dramatically to 43% and as low as only 15% for those belonging to five or more disadvantaged groups.[40]

Summary

The supply side approach of improving education, re-skilling people and investing in apprenticeships will make a significant difference to millions of people and to the economy as a whole. However, it does not address the challenges faced by the millions of poorly educated, unemployed people who live in the most deprived areas.

One of the main reasons for the poor educational performance of many children today is that their parents were the very ones who were so badly served by our education system in the eighties and nineties. I suspect that with the recent investment in schools the education system is nearing the limit of what it can do on its own for our children. If we want to push beyond these limits we have to focus more resources on the unacknowledged building blocks of children's education – their parents. I am a strong believer in the role-model effect of parenting and it is of real concern that so many parents, or soon-to-be parents, have such low levels of educational attainment.

In all the discourse about educational standards and improving schools no one ever suggests that we should compensate those people who received a poor or below-standard education. It is as if we have written them off. I suppose people are always more interested in the

40 R. Barrett, Office for National Statistics, 'Disadvantaged groups in the Labour Market', *Economic and Labour Market Review* vol. 4 no. 6, June 2010.

new topic and the fresh development than they are in the old. I saw this regularly in our second-hand furniture business – facilities managers spent ages specifying new furniture and working out where it would go, but spent hardly any time at all on planning what to do with the old furniture. We seem to think in the same way about each generation of schoolchildren. Once they have gone through the system we seem to accept our failure and turn to the next generation. This is deplorable and short-sighted. We are talking about people here, not desks. As a nation, we should be at least as concerned about those who have already left school without qualifications as we are about those children just entering the system. Improvements to the school system will not help the huge numbers of ill-educated adults who are unable to be the sort of role model that is so important to the next generation.

It is my view that we have a moral duty to make reparation to that let-down generation of poorly educated people. We should make a real and sustained effort to help them make something of their lives. We should help them to get work and to learn new skills. And we need to do it in that order: work first, then train them in the skills they need to make progress.

Aside from this moral argument, such a policy would deliver significant collateral benefits through the creation of stronger role models. If we build parents' confidence and skills through employment we will undoubtedly improve the educational outcomes of their children. Indeed, if we would only recognise the essential role that parents play in the education and development of our children we would place a much stronger emphasis on adult education, employment and training.

Chapter 10

Demand side initiatives

On the demand side, the government invests directly in measures to increase employment. One approach is Area Based Initiatives, where public investment is targeted on deprived areas with the aim of 'regenerating' them. There have been several programmes designed to achieve this. Two of the most recent were the Single Regeneration Budget and the New Deal for Communities. Another option is to create jobs through employment support measures such as New Deal or the Future Jobs Fund, whereby employers receive financial assistance to employ people. The current government has designed a new scheme of this kind called the Work Programme. A third approach is public investment in infrastructure projects such as railways, schools or roads, although the primary intention here is not to create jobs but to improve these facilities.

Area Based Initiatives (ABI): the Single Regeneration Budget (SRB), 1994–2001

The term 'Area Based Initiatives' covers a number of urban regeneration programmes designed to concentrate investment in geographically specific areas. One of the most recent was the Single Regeneration Budget (SRB). In 1994, it was established as the successor to a previous ABI scheme called City Challenge. City Challenge was a response to the riots and civil unrest of the early 1980s. In both schemes, local authorities applied to government for the funds through a competitive bidding process.

The idea was to focus the additional resources for a period of seven years in order to fulfil a number of objectives. They were to improve employment prospects, address social exclusion, promote sustainable regeneration, protect the environment and infrastructure, and support and promote economic growth. There were six rounds of SRB funding worth a total of £5.5 billion. The programme closed in 2001.

All the areas selected for SRB investment had significantly higher levels of deprivation than the national average. In the Final Evaluation Report of the SRB programme,[41] the seven case-study areas had average employment rates of only 41% as compared with the national average of 57%. Unemployment was double the national average and 28% of heads of households were unemployed against a national average of only 10%.

However, the overall impact of all this investment on employment was marginal in all the seven areas chosen for the evaluation. The training and skills agenda saw similarly unimpressive advances, as the table below (table 14.8) from the Final Evaluation Report shows:

---

41 'Evaluation of the Single Regeneration Budget: A Partnership for Regeneration', Final Evaluation Report, part 3, John Rhodesi, Peter Tyler and Angela Brennan, Department of Land Economy, University of Cambridge for the Office of the Deputy Prime Minister, February 2007.

Extract from Table 14.8: Qualifications, skills and training

| | Total 7 SRB areas | | |
	1996*	2001	change
No qualifications at all			
Head of household	50	49	-1
Any member of household	49	47	-2
Type of training received			
On-the-job	61	57	-4
Day/evening classes	32	31	-1
Govt training scheme	8	8	0

* England comparator 17% of working age population in 1996 with no qualifications falling to 16% in 1999 and 2001 (Regional Trends).

Overall the number of households without qualifications moved only in line with the national average, i.e. about 1%.

The main explanation for the disappointing rate of improvement in employment or skill levels in these areas was the lack of specific investment in training and employment. Table 14.1 below illustrates this:

Table 14.1: Total expenditure for Training and Employment by the seven case study areas (£000s)							
Theme	No projects	SRB	Other public	Private	Total	Total exp per capita	Duration (years)
Canalside Rochdale	4	619	937	423	1979	0.1	5
Chalkhill	12	3013	593	25197	28803	4.8	5
Hangleton & Knoll	1	376	181	137	694	0.1	4
Nottingham	12	2196	4564	531	7291	0.2	6
Royds Bradford	8	541	489	52	1082	0.1	7
Sunderland	2	146	586	0	732	.01	7
Swadlincote	3	29	2778	905	3712	0.1	6
Total for Theme	**42**	**6920**	**10128**	**27245**	**44293**	**0.2**	

Source: Department of Land Economy

As we see from the column 'Total exp[enditure] per capita', with the exception of Chalkhill, barely any money was allocated to the training and employment 'theme'. If Chalkhill is removed as unrepresentative the average spend per resident falls to just over £100 per resident over the course of the programme, which equates to less than £17.50 per resident per year. (Sunderland had only around £10 per resident spent on training, or £1.66 per resident per annum!)

The SRB investment often had a significant impact on the infrastructure and housing in an area, but typically it had relatively little impact on employment and training. The reason for this was that insufficient resources were allocated to training within the overall budget. In the evaluation's own words, 'Thematic schemes as a whole are not designed to tackle multiple deprivation and are rarely specifically targeted at disadvantaged households.'

Interestingly, voluntary and community groups were effectively bypassed in the SRB investment process. Again in the evaluation's own words:

> While voluntary and community groups are key to enhancing the quality of life for local people, they are often poorly resourced, too fragmented to carry out substantive regeneration activity. Although SRB was designed to encourage community involvement in local regeneration, local people did not always possess the knowledge, skills and administrative resources to be effective partners and/or lead on regeneration. Relatively small budgets within SRB (5%-7% of SRB spend) in the early years for capacity/building management and administrative expenses left limited scope and in any event lead partners/accountable bodies tended to retain this element of the funding.[42]

---

42 Evaluation of the Single Regeneration Budget: A Partnership for Regeneration – the Final Evaluation Report.

Area Based Initiatives (ABI): the New Deal for Communities (NDC), 1998

In 1998, the government introduced the New Deal for Communities (NDC) programme. Again, the focus of the NDC initiative was on areas with very high levels of deprivation. The majority (28) of the 39 chosen areas were in the most deprived decile of the Index of Multiple Deprivation. Only a small number of areas were selected to enable a concentration of resources on them. The NDC programme was to run for 10 years in each selected area.

In total £1.71 billion was spent on the NDC programme and it attracted a further £730 million of other public, private and voluntary sector resources, making a total spend of £2.44 billion.

Even though there was an increase in the level of resources deployed in each area as compared to SRB, the focus on employment was still quite marginal, and once again, the impact on employment was minimal. The Final Evaluation for the NDC initiative stated: 'When assessed against what happened in the comparator areas, there is no evidence for statistically significant net positive change in relation to worklessness.'

Table 2.4 below shows what when compared to directly comparable areas (the comparator average) where *no* investment had been made, the change in worklessness in NDC areas (NDC average) was not significant. The implication is that the rise in employment was created by the general improvement in the economy and would have happened anyway irrespective of the NDC programme.

Table 2.4: Working age employment rates			
	In employment (per cent)		
	2002	2006	Change 2002–2006
Knowsley	33.1	42.3	9.2
Newcastle	36.6	45.0	8.4
Bradford	36.0	47.8	11.8
Walsall	49.7	50.7	1.0
Newham	55.1	55.8	0.7
Lambeth	61.6	63.3	1.7
NDC average	51.5	53.6	2.1
Comparator average	58.7	60.3	1.6
National	74.8	74.6	−0.2

Source: Ipsos MORI NDC Household Survey
Base: All respondents of working age
Source national: Labour Force Survey Spring 2002; Quarter 2 (April-June) 2006
* Final column indicates 'minimum improvement' and 'maximum improvement' achieved across the 39 Partnerships, rather than 'change in minimum' and 'change in maximum'

Further analysis of the worklessness data shows that the majority of the improvement in worklessness was due to the work done with JSA (Job Seeker's Allowance) claimants.

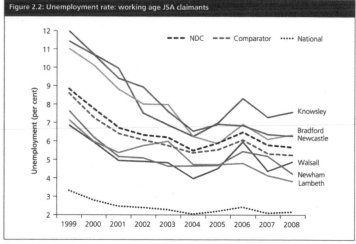

Figure 2.2: Unemployment rate: working age JSA claimants

Source: SDRC, NOMIS

Current Solutions

Once again, those furthest from the job market (and not eligible for JSA) and with the lowest chances of securing employment were left out of the programme.[43]

The report went on to analyse why so little has been achieved in terms of employment:

> Some NDCs, especially those in traditionally less buoyant labour markets, have tended to focus on, usually job-ready, JSA claimants. Other partnerships especially those in London have targeted resources on the most distanced from the labour market, or who fall outside the remit of existing mainstream provision. Health problems, a key factor in explaining the increase in economic inactivity, have not generally received a great deal of attention. Strategies have tended to focus on supply-side interventions aimed at improving the employability of residents rather than demand-side projects to stimulate economic growth. Spend varies considerably across the NDC areas, with these areas with the highest levels of worklessness tending to allocate more on worklessness interventions. With few exceptions, public sector agencies have proved to be the most cooperative partners for NDCs. By contrast, the private sector is not engaged to any great extent other than as a recipient of support or as a contracted provider of services. Some employers lack the time or the inclination to get involved but perhaps top NDCs have not always maximised opportunities for working with the private sector. There is perhaps more that could be done to understand and respond to the needs of employers. The third sector is sometimes involved in delivering services under contract or used as a channel for accessing clients but there is less evidence that it has been engaged as a strategic partner in tackling worklessness in NDC areas. This may be a missed opportunity.

---

43 'Local initiatives to help workless people find and keep paid work', Pamela Meadows, Joseph Rowntree Foundation, 26 June 2008.

The following data compares the worklessness rates for the NDC areas before the New Deal was implemented and during the period of the NDC support. It is very clear that none of the areas improved in terms of unemployment relative to the rest of the country during this period.

New comparative research on New Deal for Communities (NDC)

36 of the 39 NDC areas examined

1) Pre-New Deal context

- 24/36 NDC postcode sectors were in the top decile for JSA claims in 1985

- 26/36 were in the top decile in 1998

- More importantly, 18/36 were in the top decile every year 1985–97

- 13/36 more were in only the top two deciles 1985–97

- Only 5/36 had experienced third decile or lower at least once 1985–97

2) New Deal period (1998–2005)

- All those NDCs continuously in the top decile 1985–97 stayed there through the period 1998–2005

- 24/36 NDCs were in the top decile for every year 1998–2005

- Mean rank for all NDCs 1998–2005 was the same as 1985–97[44]

---

44 A. Fenton and R. Tunstall, 'Twenty five years and three recessions, how much difference have they made to claimant rates in high-unemployment neighbourhoods?' (2010), University of Cambridge and Centre for Analysis of Social Exclusion, Seminar Paper, London School of Economics.

The effects of ABIs

It is clear from the wealth of data that is available on Area Based Initiatives (ABIs) such as SRB and NDC that in their own terms they have been quite successful. Whole areas have been physically improved and made more attractive. Many of the people who inhabit these areas feel that they now live in a more pleasant and safer environment.

What these schemes have not done, however, is to make a significant difference to levels of long-term unemployment or worklessness. There appear to be several reasons for this lack of impact. Firstly, the resources that were devoted to employment were negligible. It was well understood that worklessness would require the investment of considerable time and effort. Despite this, it was never allocated the level of resources required to make an appreciable impact. Secondly, the solutions they offered were actually supply side solutions – skills training, CV writing, interview skills, and so on. These will help a few people who are close to employment readiness, but will not help those who are remote from work for all the reasons I outlined earlier.

The most important omission in my view was to fail to engage with the two types of organisations that can employ people: the private sector and social enterprise. It is hardly surprising that the private sector did not engage. Most small businesses focus on the job in hand, on keeping things going and maintaining the margin. They simply do not have time to consider things that are outside their remit or that may be distracting. In order to involve this sector a programme would have to spend considerable resources to reach out and demonstrate the potential benefits. On the other hand, the social enterprise community is dedicated to achieving similar goals to most ABI initiatives and many social entrepreneurs would have relished the opportunity to work closely with either SRB or NDC managers. The observation that not engaging with the third sector and social enterprise in any substantial way 'may be a missed opportunity' is absolutely accurate. Omitting to engage with the very people who have the energy, the focus and the motivation to do something tangible for long-term unemployed people is a massive missed opportunity.

Employment support measures

There have been a number of subsidised job schemes over the years. In the 1980s, almost 500,000 people were on placements under the then Conservative government's Youth Training Scheme.[45] 'Youth Training' followed this in 1989. In 1998, the Labour government introduced the New Deal programme to provide subsidies to employers who took on long-term unemployed people from a wide range of backgrounds. It was initially funded by a one-off £5 billion windfall tax on privatised utility companies. Spending on the New Deal was £1.3 billion in 2001.

There was also a New Deal for Young People (NDYP) and one for Lone Parents and others for over-25s, the disabled, for people over 50 and even for aspiring musicians. Such schemes subsidise the employment and training of long-term unemployed people (generally, those who have been unemployed for at least six months).

The NDYP began with an initial consultation session, referred to

---

45 The Youth Training Scheme (YTS) replaced the Youth Opportunities Scheme (YOP) in 1983 and became the mainstay of the national training agenda set in 1981 by the White Paper *A New Training Initiative*. Like YOP, it involved substantial (in terms of time) work experience that was intended to provide **on-the-job training**, as well as vocationally related skills training outside of the workplace. The **off-the-job** curriculum also included such transferable core skills as communication, numeracy and 'social and life skills'. Employers were subsidised by government funds. It was alleged that many trainees were gaining little valuable experience in the workplace, were being given menial or meaningless tasks, and were failing to gain real employment on completing the scheme. On the other hand, many of those involved, both organisations and trainees, claimed that it provided valuable experience and a genuine route into employment for young people. Youth Training replaced it in 1989.

as Gateway. This focused on improving job search and interview skills. If the search for employment was still unsuccessful after the Gateway sessions, a young person could only receive unemployment benefits if they chose one of these four options:

- Take a subsidised job placement. A subsidy of £60 per week was paid to the employer for six months; a £750 training allowance was also available to participating employees. The client (unemployed person) was paid a wage by the employer.

- Move into full-time education or training for up to 12 months.

- Take work in the voluntary sector. In this option, the client was paid JSA plus a £15 training allowance. This was called Community Task Force.

- Work with the Environmental Task Force. Clients were paid the equivalent of JSA. They worked full time for six months on a variety of environmental projects.

The statistics on the NDYP programme show that almost one in three (31.27%) people left the benefit system without securing a job or receiving education or training. Of the rest, 42.89% went into employment, and 25.84% stayed on benefits. During the 10 years the New Deal operated (1998–2008) it helped more than 1.8 million people into work.

New Deal was replaced in 2009 by Flexible New Deal (FND), which was in turn scrapped by the incoming coalition in 2010. Under FND, the government paid independent providers (such as charities and private companies) to try to get people back into work. The scheme applied to people who had been on the dole for more than a year. Instead of a 13-week programme, providers were to spend a year or more with each client. This was intended to give them time to get to know their clients, build rapport, and move them gradually towards work readiness. Payments were made on long-term job outcomes to encourage the providers to seek the best possible employer/client match. However, there was no mechanism for paying more money for helping clients who were harder to help. This meant that providers had a clear incentive to 'park' clients who would be expensive to help, and provide only a minimal service to them, while focusing their energies on those who could get jobs without too much support.

The scheme appeared to be extremely expensive but in an article featured in the *Daily Telegraph* entitled 'The Flexible New Deal: was it really a disaster and what can we learn from it?' (17 November 2010), journalist Neil O'Brien made these observations:

> The scheme helped 16,300 people find work, compared to a total of 279,000 people who were newly entered into it over the period. That means the cost-per-job works out at a staggering £31,284 per job. In fact, you could argue it was even worse, as only 3,870 people got a longer-term job. That *sounds* like very bad value for money. But we need a bit of context here.
>
> Firstly, because there is longer-term evidence from other countries that schemes like this have been more effective than just leaving people to turn up to job centres once in a while. Secondly, these are people who are difficult to get into jobs at the best of times. Thirdly ... the statistics ... cover the period at the bottom of the recession, from October 2009 to August this year. That was probably the hardest period in which to find someone a job in twenty years.
>
> Prodding at the statistics shows how the ratio of people enrolled into the scheme compared to people finding jobs has got steadily better as it got more established, and the economy recovered ... FND ran for such a short time it is difficult to draw any really firm conclusions.

FND recognised one of the key weaknesses of the original New Deal programme. Under New Deal, employment options typically lasted about six months, which for many people is sufficient time to help them to get into work. However, people who have been unemployed for a long time generally require a lot more help to get back into work than those made unemployed more recently. Any back-to-work or job-creation scheme should recognise that simple fact. Six months is simply not long enough for a person who has been unemployed for a considerable period to overcome the accumulated loss of social employability skills. It takes patient, steady work to help such people build their confidence and improve their skills to the standard required by modern businesses. Many will need basic literacy and numeracy skills training. All will need coaching and development in a real work environment.

The Future Jobs Fund (FJF) was different from the other employment programmes outlined here in that it focused on specific, deprived areas. Introduced in October 2009 in the depth of the recession, the £1 billion programme sought to give six months' guaranteed employment to a young person. It created a lot of jobs (150,000) very quickly in the midst of a very rapid downturn in employment. Unusually, a number of social enterprises (including GreenWorks) could apply directly to the Department of Work and Pensions (DWP) to join the scheme as employers. This meant that the employers received the full amount of the FJF payment directly from DWP with no intermediary taking its cut. This enabled employers to pay for increased supervision levels and provide tailored training for the young people. As a result, more than 50% of the young people who joined the scheme found full-time work at the end of their subsidised employment. Given that FJF was targeted at people from very deprived areas at a time of severe recession, that is a very good return indeed.

The current Coalition government's Work Programme is, according to *Telegraph* journalist Neil O'Brien, 'basically a much bigger version of FND'. The main innovation in the Work Programme is the payment by results formula. This approach means that the government only pays companies that succeed in placing clients in work for a certain period. This is very attractive to government, but there are two clear downsides: firstly it reduces the number of companies that are capable of bidding for such contracts, and secondly it means that they charge significantly more because they are taking much greater risks.

In summary most employment support measures are nothing of the sort. They should, in the main, be characterised as training support measures. Moreover, most of the training support tends to gravitate to those most able to get a job and the people who are the least able to work are not properly catered for. The mechanisms through which most of these programmes are administered are also very expensive and prevent funding from reaching the companies and other organisations that want to create genuine employment for people on the margins of society.

Chapter 11

The failure of government measures

Despite these schemes costing billions, the real needs of the long-term unemployed are not addressed by them. Outwardly, both the Area Based Initiatives and employment support measures appear to be demand side programmes aiming to create employment. However, on closer examination they are revealed as mainly supply side initiatives. It would be wrong to say that they make no difference at all – they clearly do. Millions of people have benefited from the guidance they have received and have found employment earlier than would have been the case had the assistance not existed. In the main however, the evidence suggests they supported people who were relatively close to the job market (i.e. relatively employable with reasonable skills levels) to get jobs that were likely to be created in any case. With the *partial* exception of the Future Jobs Fund, none of these initiatives created any new jobs.

The assessment systems adopted by these schemes are quite inflex-ible and they measure the wrong things. Too often, I have been obliged to count attendance on a course, or time spent in front of a computer screen, as opposed to reporting on the effectiveness of the training. At Cybercycle, we provided numeracy courses for the trainees every Thursday. They were surprisingly popular and the class responded very positively to them. One trainee told me very excitedly that he had never understood before what a million actually was: 'It's got six noughts in it!' he told me. When we told our New Deal supervisor about the course and how engaged the trainees were with it, he was more interested in how many trainees had turned up for work that day and if any of them had been late.

Their approach can be bureaucratic and top down. On one occasion at GreenWorks, when applying for some European-backed funding I had to report on the number of people I would be employing 12 months hence in a depot I had not even opened yet. Moreover, I had to predict what the distribution of the workforce would be in terms of gender, ethnic origin *and* disability!

They generally do not understand how business works or what it takes to get a business going. As witnessed by the comment in the NDC review, they struggle to work with entrepreneurial ideas and new ways of doing things. They are also extremely risk averse. This means they would rather support a classroom-based training course where they can count the number of people who attend than invest in a business looking to create new jobs with uncertain futures. The net result is that they default to supply side solutions.

Perhaps the biggest concern, though, is the reliance on intermediaries (in their parlance 'providers' or 'primes') in the process. The government in all these programmes felt that it did not have the capacity to administer such programmes and contracted intermediaries to deliver them. Almost all of these intermediaries were and are commercial organisations whose main driver is profit. It is not the profit motive per se that I object to; rather it is the cost of their intermediary role in the first place. These intermediaries are a very significant charge on the system. Under the Future Jobs Fund, the intermediaries typically received up to £2,500[46] for their role in placing each trainee. The employers who took trainees on through that intermediary received at most a few hundred pounds to cover the supervision costs. In the Work Programme, the intermediaries will receive between £4,000 and an extraordinary sum of £14,000 to find people jobs, depending on how difficult they are to place. As a result of their involvement relatively little money is deployed to where it is really needed – at the organisation that is actually employing or training the unemployed person. Under parts of the New Deal programme and now under the Work Programme, many of the charities and social enterprises doing the hard work of training receive almost nothing and in many cases literally zero.

In a revealing and thought-provoking article about the Work Programme in Hull, featured in the *Guardian* (31 January 2012), journalist Amelia Gentleman wrote:

> There's a peculiarity about the payment system here. The government money allocated for helping get people into work was meant to fund whatever external help they needed, but both the course for alcoholics, and the charity which is helping to train Cristof [one of the clients highlighted in this report], receive no money from Pertemps or G4S for helping to make him more employable. Once he gets a job, any payment will go to G4S, and Pertemps will get a cut, but the charity will not receive anything.

Many intermediaries only place the candidates who are hardest to work with through the charities and social enterprises, and work with the less difficult cases themselves. This is not only very unfair but also counterproductive. The best training, for people who have been out of work for a prolonged time, is demonstrably job based. Training delivered off-site, in a generic fashion away from the pressures

---

46 This is the profit made by the intermediaries after paying the clients (normally) minimum wage salaries.

and immediacy of work, is an ineffective diversion. The front-line employing organisations could do so much more for the trainees if they received appropriate funding to provide on-the-job training. In this way both the employing organisation and the employee would get much more from the arrangement.

Part 4

A Different Perspective

Chapter 12

The importance of work

Work creation has a multi-functional effect on our society. In addition to the wealth and health benefits that I alluded to elsewhere, I believe it is a major factor in creating a happy and active community.

Employment brings a tremendous sense of worth; it encourages others through role modelling; and it acts as a vehicle from which people will more willingly take on new skills and learning. Just the simple act of going to work brings pride and acts as a positive force. The workplace itself brings together people from different backgrounds and broadens their experience. I believe that confident people who are open to new learning and exposed to different cultures are the bedrock of a healthy society. In short, employment makes a massive contribution to social capital.

Here are some case studies drawn from my experience.

The redemptive power of employment

At Papercycle, I needed to employ a driver very urgently to cover a round the next day. I had contacted the Job Centre around midday and at 4 p.m., a slightly overweight man arrived saying he hoped the job hadn't been taken. Bert was obviously a bit desperate. He held his cap tightly in both hands and said 'Yes Boss' to everything I asked. He had not worked for months and I could see it was hurting. I was running out of time so I said he could start tomorrow at 7 a.m. and I would see him in the morning.

'Could I start at 6 a.m.?' he asked.

'No, sorry, I'll see you at 7 a.m.'

The following day went really well. Bert turned up at 7 a.m. and went off pretty briskly; he completed the round by 4 p.m. and tentatively asked if I'd need him the next day. When I said yes, he asked if he could take the van home. I declined.

The next day Bert turned up reliably and completed all the work. Very soon, his true jovial character started to shine through. Every night he asked if he could take the van home and every night I politely declined. After a few weeks, however, he got to me and I let him take the van home. A few days later, I went round to see him after work and then I understood. In pride of place outside his flat was my little van. Bert was standing there showing a neighbour his round sheet and explaining what he did. The van was clear and tangible evidence that Bert had a job – a real job. You could almost weigh the sense of pride.

Teamwork

Remember Tom Riall from Onyx? We left him wondering at the lack of respect shown by some of his customers to his team and then making a fabulous discovery about what motivates his staff – a sense of community, a sense of working together.

> Although I'd visited our depots before, I'd never been on a refuse collection round. Most of my job is confined to our London office, negotiating with clients and man-

agers in air-conditioned comfort. I'd always imagined a shift on the bins as dirty, smelly and physically hard. I was right about the last point. When I joined the early morning shift at 5.30 a.m. for a week, I had to operate at a fast pace to keep up. I'm relatively fit, luckily, and the three other guys in the crew were all very helpful. Initially, they were a bit suspicious because of my job title, but they soon accepted me.

What impressed me was the way Onyx crews and sweepers all supported each other on their rounds. When my crew ran late due to filming this programme, two other crews helped us complete our round.

Teamwork is at the heart of this story. Everyone wants to be a part of something – a family, a class, a workplace; as human beings, we need to belong. For many people I have employed over the years, the sense of being part of something seems to have been missing from their lives. When you hear their stories it is not surprising; a very poor, dysfunctional or even violent family life, often leading to poor school attendance, and almost certainly leading to poor educational attainment, leaves these people bereft of any sense of belonging. However, I have seen that change almost overnight when they get a job. For example, at GreenWorks it was a regular event to have 12 tonnes of furniture delivered on the back of a 40-foot-long articulated lorry. That is a huge quantity of furniture. It requires strength and skill to unload – and, more importantly, you need to work as a team; you cannot hide and you cannot do anything on your own when you're taking heavy desks off a trailer that stands at shoulder height to you. You need help and your colleagues need you too. Seeing a truck full of furniture turning up, helping to unload and categorise the contents and then watching it roll away empty brings a real sense of achievement. More than that, it gives a sense of achieving something with others – of being part of a team.

A vital ingredient for the creation of team spirit is a feeling of a challenge to overcome, a difficult task to complete. The workplace has a real advantage over a training programme in this. The urgency of work, the idea that time is money, is compelling. The fact that the trucks in the story above have to be turned around quickly so that they can go back to site, or that the driver is on a bonus, or that he wants to go home early creates a reality and a pressure that a training scheme simply can't replicate. The sense of reality creates a genuine need to work together as well as a sense of achievement when the truck is unloaded.

I have seen the extraordinary effect of such involvement so often it has become a mantra of mine. The effect of working with and in a team is amazing. People with apparently no confidence, who may appear completely inarticulate, can suddenly spring into life after just a few days of working.

Sense of belonging

Being the employer can be an immensely rewarding experience as well. Remember Billy, who did not know the difference between lbs and kgs? He may have had an appalling education but he was extraordinarily loyal. One day a new customer turned up with a load of paper to sell. As he was unloading, Billy came and told me he'd been offered 'a drink' if he didn't tell me that the guy had slipped a couple of very heavy RSJs (reinforced steel joists) off the truck after it had been weighed. This is a classic scam. The cheats drive onto the weighbridge and record their first weight, including a very heavy article such as an RSJ. After recording the first weight, they remove the RSJ and unload the material (in my case waste paper). They return to the weighbridge for their second weighing. The weigh-bridge records the difference between weight one and weight two and they are paid out for the 'paper' they have delivered. Once they have been paid, they put the RSJ back on the truck and drive off, having defrauded the weighbridge operator. Well, they chose the wrong guy in Billy. He was more annoyed than I was and led me down the stairs to denounce the 'customer'.

In the winter of 1994 the commodity price of paper collapsed by more than 35% overnight. I was left high and dry, unable to reduce costs on that scale in the time available. Many of the lads I employed – led by Billy – volunteered to work for nothing if it could keep the business going. It was a fantastic and humbling gesture and one that really inspired me, for it encouraged me to pick myself up and start a new business that would carry on employing people like Billy.

Recognising the value of skills

Most of the young people from challenged backgrounds whom I have employed have been unable to appreciate the value of even basic skills. To the reader it must sound amazing that children would not understand the value of being able to read or write but this is precisely the gulf in our understanding that we must try to bridge. Taking their cue from the adult role models in their lives, these young people adopt coping techniques to get by and simply do not engage with the hard work of learning because they cannot conceive the value of literacy or numeracy. However, once they do recognise the value of such skills they can show remarkable aptitude and application…

Boys' toys – the forklift truck

I went to the formal opening ceremony for our GreenWorks franchise in Scotland in 2006. It was the usual sort of event: a few speeches and then the mayor cut the ribbon and pronounced the new centre opened. It looked great; the furniture was neatly arranged and the price labels were prominently attached. All the staff, mainly young people on vocational training, were very smartly turned out in brand new, logo'd sweatshirts.

Kibble, our franchisee, is a fantastic organisation that takes children who are permanently excluded from school because they were disruptive, inattentive or too difficult to teach. Kibble works with them intensively and has a great track record of lifting their attainment in school and addressing some of the issues that they face. As part of the programme, the older children have vocational training on the job in a number of real businesses, including the GreenWorks franchise.

I got talking to one of the trainees over the lunchtime canapés that followed the speeches. Terry appeared to be very together and very coherent. He explained that he got a taxi from east of Edinburgh to Paisley every day, there and back. I asked who paid for that and he said 'the council'.

I couldn't understand why this lad was being sent to Kibble at such expense by the council and later I asked his tutor what the story was. He looked at me very hard, drew a deep breath and said, 'That boy came here six months ago and was the worst kid I've ever had in my seven years here; he was abusive, violent, and miserable – I could literally have wrung his neck many a time. Now look at him – he's a pussycat. I still canna believe it.'

I said, 'What happened?'

'Your bloody forklift, that's what happened.'

'Tell me more?'

'Well, you know that normally the lads get to come to workshops as a reward for trying at school. Well, him we sent to the scrap area just to get rid of some of his anger – you know, smashing the rubbish desks, etc. No way was he going to get to actually meet any customers or anything.'

'So what happened then?'

'Well, he saw the forklift, didn't he? – asked if he could have a go, yeah? The instructor said yes, but just pulling the levers; no moving it or anything. Well, he got on it, sent the forks up and down a bit and he just fell in love with it. He begged me to let him drive it and I told him he couldn't unless he passed a test. Of course, the big thing is that he could barely read so he'd no chance of passing. That day he started knuckling down; started to learn to read. Now he's in GreenWorks every other day driving the forklift and we wouldn't be without him – I still canna believe it!'

Crossing boundaries of discrimination

One of the groups most discriminated against in society is ex-prisoners. The taint of prison makes it incredibly difficult to get a job because its negative effects on people are profound. I believe that the difficulty of overcoming the loss of confidence and the sense of exclusion which prison inevitably creates is a fundamental cause of the high rates of recidivism that we see. When we consider that there are only about a dozen people in the whole of the prison system who will not at some point be released, it is self-evidently critical to help these people rehabilitate themselves and enable them to become contributing citizens again.

The only way to wash off the taint of prison is to enable ex-prisoners to get involved in society once more through meeting people and working with them. I have witnessed this process several times...

A thief or a driver?

The quest for drivers at Papercycle was almost never-ending. In response to one advertisement that I placed with the Job Centre, along came Jack. He was a thickset, short man who spoke well but very quietly. He was plainly quite nervous at the interview and quite anxious about something. After about 30 minutes and after getting him to locate a street on the A–Z (I had learned a lot from Gavin and Victor) and checking his driving licence (he was a qualified HGV driver), I offered him the job.

'Start tomorrow, 7 a.m.,' I said.

'That's great,' said Jack. 'But I have to tell you something first.'

'Okaaaaay,' I said warily, 'what do you need to tell me?'

'I've just got out of Brixton nick. It's my first day on the outside.'

'What were you in for?' I asked.

'Theft,' he replied.

'Well, thanks for letting me know – there's no cash handling in this job, except on the odd occasion when I tell you exactly how much you're supposed to bring back, so it's pretty difficult to do anything untoward here – do you still want to start?'

'Yes please,' said Jack.

Jack stayed with me for around three or four months and was a very good worker. One day he came in and told me he had got a job driving a 'rig' (an articulated lorry) and asked if it would be all right if he left on Friday? He was, after all, an HGV-qualified driver and the pay was a lot better as it's really skilled work, so while I was sad to see him go, I was also delighted for him. Yet another job advert with the Job Centre...

Months later, I was walking to Brixton along Coldharbour Lane, minding my own business. I vaguely noticed a huge truck marked 'Puritan Maid' coming towards me. When it came to a screeching halt right opposite me I initially thought, 'What on earth's he up to?' The next thing I knew, the driver was jumping out of the cab and crossing the road towards me – and it was Jack.

'Do you like my rig?' he asked. I said it looked superb.

He said, 'I wouldn't have got that job without you – thanks guv.' He then shook my hand and skipped back across the road, climbed back in his truck and drove off, waving as he did.

What bigger reward can there be in life?

An arsonist or a worker?

Karen was a prisoner who was on a day release scheme with us at GreenWorks (Release on Temporary Licence or ROTL). When I first met her in the prison she had the most perfect set of French nails I have ever seen. She'd trained in administration and secretarial work. She was a convicted arsonist and was doing six years for it – so no small match fire! When I told the operations manager that she was coming to work for us in the office the colour drained from his face. An arsonist? In a 35,000 sq ft warehouse, full of furniture!? Within hours, we had 'No Smoking' and 'Fire Exit' signs put up. All the fire extinguishers were checked, additional ones were ordered and safe evacuation routes were being planned. All things, frankly we needed to do anyway and now we were galvanised to do. His concern was matched by several others who expressed their reservations.

'Are you sure?' one asked.

'Should we really be employing people like that?' asked another.

'Isn't it a bit risky?' said a third.

Karen turned out to be a great worker. After a while in the office, she came to me and asked very quietly if she could see me. I said 'Of course,' and in she came to my office. She was very embarrassed at first but eventually I got her to ask her question. Do you know what she wanted? She wanted to know if she could do a stint on the shop floor breaking up the really old furniture. I laughed when she asked, and said, 'You know your nails won't survive the day, don't you?'

'I don't mind about that, I just want to have a go.'

We kitted her out that day and gave her the manual handling training and off she went. She was very safe and very thorough AND worked hard. But despite that I have to admit that I was genuinely surprised (and very pleased) that when her time came to an end and she was leaving prison and going home, three people (two of whom were the worst cynics originally!) approached me and asked if we could find her a job. One said, 'She's a real worker, she is.'

Praise indeed.

I cannot describe how happy I was and I went home with a greater spring in my step. I was so pleased for Karen. She had met deep suspicion and prejudice but she had won round the cynics through sheer hard work and good humour. Yes, I could take some credit for bringing her in to GreenWorks but she had done the hard bit – she had dealt with the prejudice and convinced people of her worth.

After Karen, we brought in a dozen more ladies (as the Prison Service refers to them) under the ROTL scheme and each of them proved herself worthy of the trust. Three of them went on to work full-time with us upon their release. That would not have been possible if they hadn't individually broken the barriers of ignorance, misconception and distrust that the label 'prisoner' engenders.

Bridging communities

A well-run workplace that is genuinely open to all comers can be a great place to break down barriers and to create what Putnam and Feldstein[47] call 'bridging capital'. It works in so many ways. Listen in to the conversation that I overheard in the canteen at GreenWorks:

'...that's what Islam is about, man – peace.'

'How can that be – you guys are always bombing people, not like Christians.'

'No, that's not right, we believe in peace, them peoples as blow people up aren't Muslims, they're nutters.'

'So what *do* you do?'

'We pray five times a day for peace and goodwill; we don't want to hurt no-one.'

'We want the same things.'

I was amazed at how earnest both parties were and how coherently they expressed their viewpoints. What also impressed me was how many people were listening intently to the conversation. At this time, we were employing upwards of 50 young people from the local area on the government's Future Jobs Fund. They came from all backgrounds and with a very wide range of skills – the

---

47 *Better Together: Restoring the American Community*, Robert D. Putnam and Lewis M. Feldstein.

only unifying qualification they had was that they'd all been on the dole for more than six months. In talking to a few of them, it was obvious that many of them had lived quite sheltered lives and had largely stayed within their communities. Working at GreenWorks was their first real experience of meeting other cultures since being at school.

The need for support

For all these reasons – wealth creation, health promotion, personal dignity, opening minds, breaking down barriers and community cohesion – work is good. However, we should remember that those who have been unemployed for a prolonged period, or who live in areas where the culture of work is absent, need a lot of support in order to find and then secure employment.

Chapter 13

Patient employment

Increased employment will have a measurable impact on a deprived area. However, it will not achieve a transformational effect unless it is supplemented by work-based experiential training and learning. This then begs the following two questions:

How will we train and up-skill adults who have been so badly served by the education system?

How can we turn them into positive role models?

To do that we need to create what I call 'patient employment' for adults as well as for young people. By 'employment', I mean a real job with real priorities and real deadlines. By 'patient', I mean a job where the employer has some empathy with the challenges faced by long-term unemployed people and is willing to invest time and energy in working with them.

A patient employer would be tolerant of the lack of social employability skills for the first few weeks or so. A patient employer would promote basic skills training (literacy, numeracy and social skills) and actively encourage staff to learn new skills. This combination of tolerance and encouragement is crucial if we are to encourage older adults to engage with learning and take on new skills.

The quote below demonstrates what can be achieved by working patiently with discouraged people. Neil had been unemployed for more than a year when he started work at GreenWorks. The course he refers to was an NVQ2, which he did pass.

Completing my work experienc at GreenWorks Has contributed towards me possibly passing my course, and I thank GWs for making this possible. I enjoyed my time here and is happy for the opportunity to I had to work with the warehouse team and experiencing being involved with them doing a good thing with the office furniture equiptment that was delivered to The warehouse.

I have done similar work like this in the past and I have learned that I still have the energy and ability to can do this sort of work.

Neil's words demonstrate that most people's horizons rise incrementally and not in leaps. This is what E. F. Schumacher was alluding to when he said that work must stand in *some organic relationship* to what the community knows.

For instance, at first, the three lads from south Tyneside mentioned in chapter 8 just wanted to get off the dole. They had no understanding or belief that the course at Renew was anything other than a way of earning some money. However, after a few weeks, they started to appreciate what was on offer. Once they saw the opportunities that our work-based training could give them they started taking a very active interest in how the programme was working for them. Gradually they started to take responsibility for how the whole factory operated, and to get involved in supervising new trainees, and so on.

The following quote from a young woman who joined Green-Works is another example of how the work environment can promote learning:

> I hadn't been working for several months and was getting restless, but since GreenWorks I have been more energetic. I'd worked in an office before, just filing, but I've learnt a lot in the few months I have been here; I have learnt how to use Microsoft Excel and Outlook. I am now more confident in what I do and I like answering the phone and talking to customers either over the phone or face-to-face.

However, where people have very limited experience of work you have to build that organic relationship from scratch. We saw in the story of the lad who refused to make the tea that there are people who do not understand the concept of progression and development at work. They imagine that the job they do on day one will be the job they do from then on. We use expressions like 'climbing the ladder' or 'getting on the first rung'. I have met many people who do not know that the ladder even exists, let alone that they can climb it. It takes a lot of patient guidance to get such people to understand and believe in the presence of the ladder.

Training is most effective when three vital elements are present. Potential trainees have to understand the need for, or the relevance of, the training; they have to want to learn; and they learn best through action – by doing things themselves.

People generally engage with training where they see a real need for it. That is true of all classes and types. All of us have experienced being sent on a course for something we do not know about and don't regard as central to our jobs. We didn't take it too seriously, didn't really focus on the skills on offer, and treated the training as a break from the day-to-day. Contrast that with the experience of learning something we needed to know and which improved our prospects. On those courses, we were focused, engaged and keen. It is no different for ill-educated people from deprived communities. Once you pique a person's interest the best way to learn is experientially – on, or related to, the job.

The computer whizz-kids

Remember the two lads in Brixton Job Centre who didn't want to wear high heels? This is what happened when I asked if they would like a course on *fixing* computers. They looked up for the first time, raised their eyes and fixed us with a smile – 'Yeah man, we'd like that!'

They duly started the next week and within four weeks, they were able to assess, fault-find and fix any PC. They had both experienced that nerve-racking moment when, under test conditions, having found and rectified a fault, they faced the acid test – would it actually work? And they had both passed that test. Their confidence was booming and they wanted to sell the computers they were fixing – they knew they had done a good job and these units were worth something. We held an impromptu meeting with the whole team about how we could sell the computers.

One of the first things someone said was that we would need to create labels that told customers what the specification was, what we'd done to each computer to make it work and how they were really good value. They knew all the phrases to throw in – 'good value', 'great operation', 'fantastic bargain', etc. At the end of the meeting, I left them to get on with laying out a showroom and creating some labels. The next day one of the two lads whom we'd interviewed came into my office and asked me, without any irony: 'Can we get a course on word processing so we can learn how to do labels and fancy borders?' No mention of high heels now.

All this means that the job comes first and the skills acquisition follows. Therefore, the schemes that focus on skills *before* jobs have it the wrong way round. If we continue to send people for training for jobs that don't exist or which from their point of view seem out of sight, even if they do the training, we will continue to waste not only millions of pounds but also lots of good people's lives.

Karen Lowthrop from Hill Holt Wood supports this view.[48] She and her husband Nigel share a philosophy that practical training can build self-esteem. Their woods-based skills programme is currently helping more than 250 young men who are permanently excluded from school to rebuild their self-esteem. The programme is very popular and the boys who go on it show a real change in attendance and attention. Karen is very direct and clear about the process: 'The system is blinkered, it wants accredited learning from the start but you have to get *to* the boy first. Formal won't work – doesn't work; they need informal learning.'

When all three training elements are assembled, incredible progress will be made. I saw real learning with Terry on the forklift, I saw it with the lads who did not want to wear high heels to work, and I saw it again with Billy and his scales. I saw it dozens of times at GreenWorks. I really believe that we have to create the jobs first and then train people in the skills for those jobs. Just like at Westfield shopping centre – if someone from a marginalised group gets a real job they will adapt and learn what is required to do that job. People respond better to training and learn much more when they see the relevance of it.

The Centre for Analysis of Youth Transitions also supports this

---

48 Karen's story is incredible. She left a well-paid corporate job to spend 10 years living in a cramped caravan with her husband Nigel, working for what she believed in. Today Hill Holt Wood is one of the most respected social enterprises in the country. It is helping hundreds of deprived boys who have been permanently excluded from school to fit back into the community.

view. In its December 2011 report, 'Young people's education and labour market choices aged 16/17 to 18/19', it stated:

> In the medium and longer term, outcomes for those taking jobs without training were generally not significantly different from those who took jobs with training. Our analysis therefore implies that simply taking a job with training is not sufficient to guarantee better labour market outcomes. To secure higher earnings, young people need training with progression which leads them to acquire an economically valuable qualification.[49]

If one of the keys to effective learning is finding things that interest people then the key to tackling worklessness will be to create genuine diversity of opportunity. We need a wide range of jobs and volunteering places that people can engage with and where they can make a difference. The jobs and places need to be of a nature that individuals can identify with and that *stand in some organic relationship* to their current situation. It is important that they really believe they can do the job because the fear of failure is very strong in people whose confidence is at a low point.

In 2009, GreenWorks won a contract under the last government's Future Jobs Fund (FJF). The fund was set up to support unemployed young people living in deprived areas by offering *paid* placements of 25 hours per week for six months. We offered 79 such placements to the FJF scheme because we were open to the idea of letting them gain experience anywhere in the business. So we had people in finance, credit control, HR, telesales, operations, manufacturing, stock management, repairs, goods preparation, deliveries, goods-in, recycling, etc. We were able to fill all the posts very quickly because we had something that would appeal to everyone. Moreover, we could offer the opportunity for people to 'taste' certain activities for

---

49 'Young people's education and labour market choices aged 16/17 to 18/19', Claire Crawford, Kathryn Duckworth, Anna Vignoles and Gill Wyness, Centre for Analysis of Youth Transitions, December 2011.

a few weeks to see if they liked them or not. Many of them changed jobs mid-programme, either because we saw they had a talent or because they saw something that interested them. The number of people who started on the shop floor and progressed successfully into sales or finance roles was staggering. Most of the trainees went through an NVQ training programme as part of their placement.

Here is some of the feedback we got from the trainees:

> I was in and out of work for three years when I was given the opportunity to work as a Merchandiser for GreenWorks. GreenWorks has a friendly environment with a hardworking but not stressful atmosphere. I was trained in manual handling by the company which will benefit me in jobs in the future. I also gained more experience driving a forklift which will be of benefit to me when applying for warehouse jobs.

> I have benefited from being with GreenWorks as it has enabled me to see that hard work pays off, as every item of furniture I sell enables the company to be more successful and do better on a monthly basis. GreenWorks has given me direct face-to-face sales experience, which I have had previous experience of, but not on a regular basis. My time at GreenWorks has also enabled me to learn how to deal with difficult customers, and ensure they leave satisfied with the service they have received. GreenWorks is a working environment in which your line managers are strict but fair when encouraging you to meet targets and get the job done.

> If it wasn't for GreenWorks and the invaluable opportunity it provided me during a time when opportunities were scarce, I truly doubt that I would have secured my current permanent position [as a Human Resources executive]. Working for GreenWorks has not only provided me with the opportunity to gain entry into the field in which I hope

to build a successful career, but enabled me to build my confidence and develop many work-related skills which have aided my professional development.

If we look back at Karen's story (the first lady prisoner to work at GreenWorks), she did not really know what kind of work suited her. She had set her mind on administration but actually did not like it. It turned out that she preferred practical work and being at the sharp end of things. Many people, especially from communities where there is a high proportion of worklessness, don't have any reference points or understand what work entails generally, let alone what a specific job involves. To get them engaged you have to be able to offer real variety so they can discover what inspires them.

Chapter 14

Employment in deprived areas

The focus on supply side solutions has resulted in a major failure to create work for the millions living in areas of severe deprivation and who are unemployed or under-employed. We need a change of approach; we need a demand side approach that deliberately sets out to create new jobs.

A report into research carried out by the Institute for Employment Studies (IES) for the Department for Work and Pensions[50] concluded, 'policy interventions which are restricted to advice, guidance, confidence building and motivational encouragement (or indeed to sanction, penalty and retribution) are unlikely to be sufficient to make significant quantitative inroads into workless communities'. The authors went on to say, 'Policy measures encouraging employment which are restricted to the individual may well be undermined by family or communal pressures, suggesting they

---

50 'Understanding Workless People and Communities, a literature review', Helen Ritchie, Jo Casebourne and Jo Rick, DWP Research Report 255, IES, June 2005.

should be clustered in ways that affect both individuals and their social network.'

This research chimes consistently with the feelings of the people who live in these deprived areas. They want to work but there are not enough jobs around for which they are qualified. When suitable jobs are advertised they attract up to 50 applicants for each one.

In order to help these people to get into work and start to develop new skills, we need to create new jobs. Currently, we seem to believe that this is not really possible. We seem to have given up on creating low-skilled jobs – everything must be high-tech, requiring advanced skills. I disagree and I will show that it is possible to create meaningful but accessible jobs for the people who need them.

By directly creating new jobs in deprived areas, we will immediately relieve some of the most appalling effects of multiple deprivation. Even more importantly for the long term, by creating the jobs first we will engender an interest and engagement in training in basic and social employability skills. This is a far more effective route to addressing the supply side issue of low overall skill levels.

In striving to create jobs in deprived areas we must not forget the warning in the IES report: we must also address the social and communal issues that afflict these areas.

Social capital and the element of trust

In their book, *Better Together*, Putnam and Feldstein look at how to create communities where there is trust and where people from widely differing backgrounds can work, live and socialise together. They point out that it is vitally important to establish two types of social capital to enable a community to function well: *bonding capital*, which they define as 'ties that link individuals or groups that have much in common – gender, age, ethnicity, and upbringing', and *bridging capital*, defined as 'ties that link individuals across a greater social distance that don't have much in common'.

They point out that bonding capital is by definition much easier to establish than bridging capital. It is typically created in communities where people know each other, share common social and cultural bonds and speak a common language. In diverse communities such as those which are typical of our inner cities, bridging capital is the most precious and elusive form of social capital. It is much harder to create in any circumstances, but inequality and deprivation reduce trust within a community and compound this inherent difficulty. The evidence available suggests that trust, a vital element of social capital, has declined in our most deprived inner city communities.

In 2011, the new Secretary of State for Work and Pensions, Iain Duncan Smith, produced a 'State of the nation report: poverty, worklessness and welfare dependency in the UK'. In it, he reported survey data that showed, 'only half of people feel that people in their neighbourhood can be trusted, with trust lowest among those aged 16–25 years (33%) *and those in the most deprived areas [at only] 21%*' (my italics).

This is a very worrying statistic. The fact that only one person in five thinks his neighbours can be trusted will inevitably reinforce several negative aspects of life in that community. It increases anxiety levels and the fear of crime and possibly even increases crime itself. It also reduces the capacity for that community to cooperate together over issues of common concern. Where trust is low, it is very difficult to build community organisations that can work together to tackle issues and problems in the area. In their book, *The Spirit Level,*[51] Richard Wilkinson and Kate Pickett have identified that a loss of trust in society reduces general health levels and increases feelings of insecurity for the *whole* population.

The fact that so many areas of the UK suffer very high levels of deprivation and a consequent loss in trust should therefore be a cause for concern for everyone.

---

51 *The Spirit Level: Why Equality is Better for Everyone,* Richard Wilkinson and Kate Pickett.

A Different Perspective

Chapter 15

Building real jobs and social capital

The areas that feature in the lowest deciles of the Index of Multiple Deprivation (IMD) face an incredible combination of what appear to be intractable issues. Crime rates are high, health is poor, families are more fragmented, unemployment rates are high and overall income is very low. The cause-and-effect relationship between these issues is effectively circular. While I believe that worklessness is at the heart of the problem, it would be naive to suggest that job creation is the answer to all the problems in these areas. Indeed, in order to enable people to take up the jobs that we create, a considerable amount of support will be required.

The state can only provide limited help in tackling these issues. The community itself has the best answers and policy should aim at encouraging people to set up organisations and groups that have the inspiration and the energy to put those answers into practice. By galvanising and encouraging a self-help attitude, many people from all parts of the community will be attracted to join in and help.

How to create real jobs in challenged areas

To go back to my original challenge set out in chapter 5 – how can we create jobs for those who have been unemployed for a long time in areas that are conditioned to high levels of unemployment? And how can we address some of the intractable social problems that exist side by side with worklessness in those areas? Is there a magic formula that has so far eluded policy-makers?

We already observed part of the answer in our brief examination of Area Based Initiatives (ABIs) in chapter 10. The philosophy underpinning ABIs recognises that deprivation is highly concentrated and emphasises the need to focus resources on specific areas of need. Patience is also critical to success. The Final Evaluation of the Single Regeneration Budget (SRB) programme concluded that: 'Bringing about strong and lasting solutions to regeneration problems at the local level requires a commitment over many years. [Such programmes] work by making a continued, relatively small but significant, contribution that has a cumulative effect.'

We also saw in the reviews of both the SRB and New Deal for Communities (NDC) programmes that the investments under both of those programmes had been spread thinly across a number of objectives. The lesson must be that in addition to patience and focus we need to concentrate on a much narrower range of objectives, i.e. relieving worklessness and building a community support infrastructure.

In addition to patience, geographical focus and a concentrated approach to worklessness and community capacity, I have shown that we need to offer diversity of opportunity. An economist would call this 'clustering' – the idea of bringing a large number of diverse but mutually supportive industries together in one area.

The theory of climax ecology

Elzéard Bouffier believed in clustering. He patiently and single-mindedly planted a variety of trees over a long period and gradually changed the landscape. He planted different species in different parts of the valley depending on the conditions he found. As his trees grew, they created the conditions for other plants to grow and gradually the land became healthier again. Ecologists have a theory for this that chimes really well with the concept of building a community.

Climax ecology is a theory first put forward by an ecologist called Frederic Clements (1874–1945). He saw that where a bare surface becomes available for colonisation by plants, the vegetation that lives there will pass through a succession of so-called 'seral stages', as more complex plant and animal communities replace the earlier, simpler ones. Ultimately, a state of equilibrium or climax is reached, which will reflect the type of climate, soil or human activity that is present.

We see it in derelict sites all around us. The most obvious early plant that grows in derelict patches of ground is the buddleia, and then often close behind it comes the ash. The oak and the ash are colonising species because of their ability to grow in difficult conditions. As they grow and thrive, they create shade and soil mass for other plants to establish. As these new plants develop, so in turn do others.

As the plant community grows, it develops an ever-widening range of niches in which more diverse wildlife can thrive. The developing eco-system brings a wide range of benefits. The roots of the trees lock in more moisture and the rain does not just run off the landscape. The trees produce leaves every autumn that fall and gradually rot to become fantastic soil conditioner. The leaves and the moisture provide homes for an extraordinary range of small invertebrates, which in turn become food for creatures higher up the food chain such as birds and small mammals. The increased shade and the improved soil are perfect for berry-bearing shrubs that provide food for yet more creatures. And so the process goes on.

The missing link

We are starting to see a formula come together, but we are still missing one vital ingredient. One of the biggest omissions noted by the NDC review and typical of other ABIs was the failure to engage with the private or the social enterprise sectors.

What sort of businesses should we encourage to cluster in areas of intense worklessness? Private or social enterprise?

What would Elzéard Bouffier recommend? Well, he would tell us to plant those species which thrive in adverse conditions and which want to settle amidst them. In a business sense, what would be the equivalents of the ash or the buddleia? What sort of business would deliberately invest in a very deprived area with the intention of employing people who very few others would even interview? What sort of business would be willing to offer the sort of patient employment model that I am advocating?

In the next part of the book, I will demonstrate why the answer must be: social enterprises. The people that run them, the social entrepreneurs, are the pioneers – the colonising species that will actively seek to plant themselves in difficult areas where others will not invest. As their businesses grow and develop, so, gradually, will the local economy. As the local economy grows, so pride in the neighbourhood and trust in its inhabitants will follow. Just as the diversity of plants and animals grows in climax ecology, so will the growing local economy create the conditions that will attract new investment and more (and different) jobs will be created.

Social entrepreneurs come in all shapes and sizes but they have one singular thing in common: they want to use their business to create real, tangible benefits for people and communities, and to change lives in a positive way.

We now have a complete formula for tackling worklessness in deprived areas: intense long-term planting of social enterprises in defined areas of worklessness, which will create real employment and improve social cohesion.

What is a social entrepreneur?

There are many definitions of the term social entrepreneur, but I have a very simple one: 'a person who uses entrepreneurial skills for the primary purpose of resolving difficult social or environmental issues'.

On the ground, the term encompasses a very wide range of individuals. It includes:

- people who run fully constituted businesses providing services to customers to very high ethical standards, who reinvest *all* the profits back into the business to do less economically viable things such as train young people. GreenWorks would be a good example of this approach;

- those who run businesses that seek to maximise profits, and at the end of the year transfer those profits entirely to a charity. A good example of this would be Oxfam Trading, whose shops make a profit which is donated to the holding charity every year; and

- people who want to get things done in a community and who use entrepreneurial methods to achieve them. Examples of this include youth clubs and community groups whose funding comes from a mixture of sources, including selling refreshments or charging members a subscription, as well as the traditional application to local authorities for funding.

The *key* thing about a social entrepreneur is that they want to use business methods to make a difference, not for them personally, but for the wider society. They do not measure themselves in terms of profit but rather by the impact they have on the issue with which they are concerned.

It is the very diversity of entrepreneurs that makes a programme of investing in social enterprise so powerful in the relief of poverty and the reversing of disadvantage. Such a strategy involves backing people who really understand what the issues are, care intensely about them, and have the energy and commitment to change things.

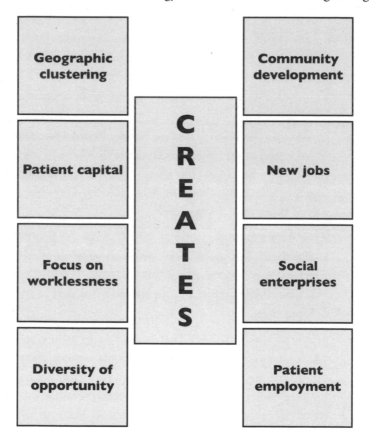

A Different Perspective

Some examples of social enterprise

I founded **GreenWorks** in 2000 to address what I saw as a market failure. Large companies were dumping huge quantities of perfectly good office furniture, while charities and other not-for-profit groups were making do with poor quality furniture. The work of collecting, grading, cleaning, repairing, selling and then reinstalling the furniture is very labour intensive. By setting up GreenWorks, I could address a market failure, prevent furniture from going to landfill and help many small charities while creating work for less skilled people.

Renew North East is a registered charity that specialises in recycling and refurbishing electrical appliances for resale to the public or to the trade at greatly reduced prices. The revenue gained from the resale allows for the development of varied training programmes for our technicians. Trainees receive practical paid work experience, which enables them to obtain NVQ qualifications and increases their likelihood of gaining full-time employment upon completion of the course.

Originally, Renew concentrated on refurbishing large electrical appliances such as washing machines, tumble dryers, cookers, fridges and freezers, including makes such as Hoover, Hotpoint and Zanussi. However, responding to popular demand and the need to offer more advanced training for the technicians, Renew has widened its service to include the resale of small electrical items such as hairdressing equipment, kettles, irons, toasters, vacuum cleaners, sun beds, deep fat fryers, juicers, food processors and so on. Every item sold has a six-month guarantee and is of exceptionally high quality, making Renew stand out from other providers.

Nigel and Karen Lowthrop purchased **Hill Holt Wood** in 1995. The wood was in poor condition, with invasive rhododendron and a damaged drainage system. The previous owners had removed most of the quality timber. In 1997, the Hill Holt Wood project established a link between the new owners and the surrounding community of 10,000 people. When Karen and Nigel set up a wood-based training business, the social enterprise was born. They have used the ethos of low impact forest management and respect for the environment to create a special learning space for young people who have experienced huge problems in their lives. Hill Holt Woods provides accessible and tactile learning to excluded schoolchildren, young offenders and unemployed or otherwise disadvantaged young people. Very subtly but effectively they are helping them become employable.

Hectic2010 In Air Enterprise Ltd is a social enterprise offering a training programme aimed at bringing long-term employment to young adults in the Barking, Dagenham and Redbridge area. Its activities include the installation of CCTV and the planning and building of monitoring rooms; installing burglar and fire alarms; and block wiring of new builds in the construction industry.

Multitaska is a business established to offer other organisations, big and small, outsourcing solutions to enable them to thrive. How they operate is very different to other businesses offering similar services. In their words:

'We are an enterprise with a social conscience. 50% of our workforce has learning disabilities. But our clients don't hire us out of the goodness of their hearts. They hire us because of the unique attributes our people contribute to their businesses. Our people are highly motivated, flexible and dedicated. They have the ability to apply themselves to all kinds of tasks, with more enthusiasm and gusto than many other people. What is more, they take delight in their work, and it shows. In return for

A Different Perspective

being the heart and soul of our business, the people we employ with learning disabilities get to earn a fair living, become more integrated into society and enjoy fuller and happier lives.'

'Cycle into Work' is an innovative training and employment programme developed and piloted by **Bikeworks**. The programme delivers work-based vocational training placements and employment opportunities for homeless and ex-homeless people. Participants have the opportunity to gain accredited professional qualifications in bicycle mechanics and national standard cycle instruction.

Chapter 16

Social entrepreneurs

Social entrepreneurs are optimists and they are innovators. They think things need to change and they think they can change them.

If you meet a social entrepreneur, you will notice some core characteristics:

- They focus on the change they want to see. They have a clear idea, based on personal experience, of what people in their community really want and they are determined to provide it.

- They are persistent. This is an outstanding feature of almost every social entrepreneur's story. Despite the fact that they often struggle to get a hearing or to generate interest among businesses or public bodies, they keep trying and carry on networking. They know there are other people in the world who not only agree with them but will also support them – the trick is finding them. In my lectures to budding social entrepreneurs, I often say, 'There are a few princes out there who can help but you will have to kiss a lot of frogs to find them!'

- They have the ability to speak in different languages for different audiences, and to translate between the two or sometimes three parties involved in a project. First, they can communicate with their community; they are often well known and respected locally. Second, they can talk with the local authority and use the language familiar to council officers. They know all the acronyms and jargon the council uses, and can apply them appropriately. In my case I also had to learn the language of the corporate world and couch my pitches to them in a 'business speak' that would have been completely out of place in the warehouse.

- They tend to remind me of Bernard Shaw's 'unreasonable man'. He famously wrote: '*The reasonable man adapts himself to the world; the unreasonable one persists in trying to adapt the world to himself. Therefore all progress depends on the unreasonable man.*'[52]

Social entrepreneurs build social capital

The solutions to these entrenched problems are multi-layered, and in areas suffering low levels of trust (where as few as one person in five will consider their neighbours trustworthy), there will be challenges in getting the community to work together. It is not enough simply to engender bonding in the workplace; we need to bring communities together socially as well.

In their book, *Better Together* (mentioned in chapter 14), Robert D. Putnam and Lewis M. Feldstein describe many strategies for building both bonding and bridging capital.

Two different strategies seem to be necessary to create these two

---

52 George Bernard Shaw, *Man and Superman* (1903).

very different types of social capital. Putnam is clear that to create strong bonding capital, small-scale, face-to-face engagement works best even though this approach clearly takes more time. Developing such bonds also runs the risk of creating narrow communities where a small group can become quite parochial. To widen these bonds and to create genuine community cohesion requires a wider kind of engagement: bridging capital.

Putnam and Feldstein assert that bridging capital thrives where community organisations can exercise power and influence. They identify the essential criteria for organisations to achieve power and influence as being both a critical mass of people and diversity of membership.

To begin with, says Putnam, 'Critical mass creates an energy that attracts people and gets change happening. It is involving and people will want to be part of it.' We can all recognise that from our own experience. Success breeds success. Successful football teams attract more supporters, even supporters from areas well beyond their home base – the classic 'prawn sandwich eaters' jibe about Manchester United fans comes to mind. In this way, they grow support and increase the diversity of that support.

In a democracy, the size of a given community can be a very powerful factor. If there is a lot of local support for a particular campaign, the authorities tend to sit up and take notice. I saw that very clearly when I signed up as a member of the management team of a small Friends organisation for our local park. The park is right on the boundary of another local authority and more than half of its regular users do not come from our borough. It was a classic example of the 'core–periphery effect' whereby authorities take a lot less notice of areas and communities on their periphery than they do of those at the core of their territory.

I cannot say I played a huge role but I helped to get that Friends group to be more active. We leafleted, we networked, and gradually as a group we gained quite a large membership. We found some very active people who started to contact the council more and more often about 'our park'.

Within 12 months, we had put ourselves on the map and the officers who responded to us were very clear about why they did so. Yes, we had made a lot of noise, but councils see (and hear) many groups that make a noise. What impressed them most was the fact that we had developed a demonstrable support base from across the community. As a large and diverse group we now had the ear of the council. Over the next year, we attracted a whole variety of funds – some from disability access budgets, some from regeneration and some from the maintenance budget – and in that short time we got the toilets fixed, the bandstand repaired and a new flower garden planted.

This is a classic example of the power to negotiate with authority that size can give a community. This applies across all public bodies or public service providers, whether they are health authorities, the police or the railway company. Size counts. The power goes further than just lobbying; it also enables and encourages higher levels of investment. There is no doubt that the council in this case agreed to invest resources in upgrading the park because of the size and diversity of the group seeking that investment.

In business, too, we can see the same effect. Where there is an identifiable community and a sense of local pride, businesses will invest – new shops open, old shops are refurbished and new services are attracted. One investment begets another. In this way, it is possible to reverse the gradual decline of an area.

One of the mistakes noted in the SRB (Single Regeneration Budget) evaluation (chapter 10) was that the SRB authorities themselves spent most of the very limited funds earmarked for developing the capacity of community groups. This not only demonstrated a lack of trust in the communities that they were being paid to help but also cut off any chance of that community developing its capacity to organise itself once the SRB finished. A centrepiece of any new ABI (Area Based Initiative) schemes should therefore be long-term direct investment into supporting local organisations and the social entrepreneurs who lead them. They are the people who are best placed to spend money and direct investment in ways that will create the most benefit for their community.

It is essential, too, to invest in local people whose objectives are less commercial. Some excellent work has been done on building communities and one of the best examples of that is the work exemplified by Andrew Mawson, in his book, *Social Entrepreneur – Making Communities Work*.[53] He knows what it takes to build a community. He says,

> It was very clear to me that it was in forging relationships between people from different backgrounds that progress was to be made; *in people willing to 'learn by doing' and engage in practical activity together in an area over a long period of time* [my italics] – getting stuck into the detail – rather than focusing solely on rhetoric and long-winded debate.

Andrew describes how, by taking a business-like approach to solving problems and to understanding the 'market', a social entrepreneur can make the system work for the community and can make things happen to transform the effectiveness of public services, from health through to education.

Putnam and Feldstein are very clear that stories have a special power to unify and bond. They can also make a powerful impression on potential investors and funding organisations wishing to put their money where it has most hope of achieving something tangible.

Over time, the community will create its own stories and folklore. In Montreal, for instance, there is a small company called Pirogue that specialises in researching and writing company histories – really delving into their past and understanding what the founders stood for and how they overcame challenges and difficulties, not just the dry histories of accounts and balance sheets. By

---

53 Andrew Mawson is best known for his pioneering work at the Bromley by Bow Centre in East London, which became the UK's first Healthy Living Centre. The Bromley by Bow Centre is a community organisation which encompasses an array of integrated social enterprises based around art, health, education and practical skills. Mawson received an OBE in the Millennium New Year Honours List for his work there since 1984.

　　　　　　　　　　　　　A Different Perspective

providing a narrative that companies can adopt, France Lord, the proprietor, says: 'knowing the history of something gives everyone, staff and managers alike, a sense of perspective. We've noticed that everyone perks up when they realise that they are playing a part in a much bigger story.'

I think that this process can be encouraged and nurtured in a community. As Andrew Mawson found in Bromley by Bow, there is an incredible amount of creative energy in even the most deprived communities and it will quite dramatically emerge if given the opportunity to express itself.

Social enterprises and voluntary organisations (like the Friends group for my local park mentioned above) are already very active in the field of community engagement in many areas. However, as the research by the Third Sector Research Council (TSRC) reported below suggests, there are significantly fewer voluntary organisations working in deprived areas than in better-off communities.

DEPRIVED LOCAL AREAS HAVE FEWER VOLUNTARY ORGANISATIONS

September 2011

Research from the TSRC reveals that more deprived areas of the country have a lower prevalence of voluntary organisations than less deprived ones. The research estimated the numbers of registered third sector organisations working at the neighbourhood level, in different kinds of local areas according to a measure of multiple deprivation. *Overall, it found that poorer areas had about 40% of the number of organisations, per head of population, than the least deprived areas.*[54]

---

54 'Voluntary sector organisations working at the neighbourhood level in England: patterns by local area deprivation', by David Clifford, Third Sector Research Council.

There are plenty of concerned and organised people living in these areas who could set up and run community organisations for local benefit. However, as we have noted already, the challenges of everyday survival seem to reduce levels of trust in deprived communities to very low levels. Poor education standards also inhibit the development of viable community organisations in deprived areas and make them much harder to set up and organise.

As a local councillor, I attended a meeting of a community youth group to guide them in their application to the council for 'Community Chest' funding. The group had a proven track record of working with local young people during the holidays and had a clear idea of what they wanted to do with any funding they secured. Their challenge was that they found the application form difficult to understand and they did not know how to complete it. However, as we discussed how to prepare the application, it transpired that there was another problem. No one in the group could use the donated word processor and it had never even been switched on!

Many quite effective voluntary groups and small social enterprises are not able to produce financial records or follow governance procedures to the standard required by the local council. I have witnessed scenes of mutual incomprehension where community groups meet council officers to discuss these standards. The community groups feel oppressed by stifling bureaucracy and the officers are frustrated by what they view as incompetence.

There is a clear need to promote the development of more community and voluntary groups in deprived areas. Local authorities should adopt a proactive and coordinated programme to assist those residents who have the energy and motivation to improve their area. In order for such a programme to be successful though, councils need to strike a better balance between the support that they provide and the restraints they place on organisations. Rather as a parent needs at some point to let its child go out on its own, so a council needs to trust its communities more. They need to be allowed to make their own judgements and learn from their mistakes. In this way they will develop much greater resilience and self-reliance.

Are there enough social entrepreneurs?

As I write, there are thousands of social enterprises across the country recruiting and employing people who have experienced the most extraordinary social disadvantages. Unlike most commercial organisations, they deliberately seek to employ such people and to help them overcome their challenges. They do it without many thanks, on incredibly tight budgets and with little reward. They operate in every town and city, making a difference locally and helping as many people as they can.

However, these social enterprises are spread thinly around the country. One or two trees in an area do not make a wood, and they are a long way short of a thriving, exciting, diverse and fertile forest. As a result, their impact on any area is limited.

Fortunately, thousands of budding entrepreneurs are seriously considering setting up a business with the social enterprise model. Of the 2 million people who want to start their own business, one in eight (11.9%)[55] say they want to set up as a company limited by guarantee, which is the most popular legal structure for a social enterprise. That is 238,000 people, with energy and passion about an issue, who want to start a social business!

The enthusiasm is there for this approach to business and for getting things done. The key now is to adopt the right policies that will encourage these social entrepreneurs to cluster with other social enterprises so that they can have the maximum effect.

---

[55] UK Department for Business, Innovation and Skills (BIS) data.

Chapter 17

Why social enterprise?

As I started to think about this book, I discussed the ideas in it with friends and business acquaintances. One question in particular came frequently from those people whose experience was outside social enterprise: 'What is wrong with the market? Surely if a service is needed the market will provide it. Someone will invest locally; set up a shop or whatever and provide that service.'

My reply is that while there is indeed some money to be made in the deprived areas at the centre of this book, the market goes where margins are higher and where investments are likely to make greater returns. Many business people would not invest in areas where crime is high and skill levels are low, and which are less attractive to potential employees from outside the area.

Social enterprises, on the other hand, are motivated by precisely those challenges. They are deliberately created to tackle ingrained and difficult social issues. They are not focused on profit maximisation as a first priority. As a result, they will often be set up in areas where the challenges are greater and the margins probably lower.

In their most recent report, 'Fightback Britain' (2011), Social Enterprise UK[56] researchers found that 39% of social enterprises are established in the most deprived 20% of local authority wards (IMD Bands One and Two) whereas less than a third of that proportion (13%) of commercial SMEs (an EU term for small and medium enterprises)[57] will be located in those areas. The researchers found that these social enterprises are locating in deprived areas precisely *because* in those areas they can have the greatest effect. When they asked about each social enterprise's objective, they discovered that 30% of the social enterprises located in Band One deprived areas are dedicated to tackling chronic unemployment and creating work for those who have struggled in the past. A further 25% stated that 'improving their community' was their first priority.

Distribution of business types by IMD bands

	Band One	Band Two	Band Three	Band Four	Band Five
% social enterprises	39	24	17	11	9
% start-up social enterprises	32	27	10	13	10
% SMEs	13	18	23	24	23

---

56 SEUK is the national body representing social enterprises. It provides advice on starting up or growing a social enterprise and campaigns in support of the concept of social enterprise. Check them out at www.socialenterprise.org.uk

57 Enterprises qualify as micro, small and medium-sized enterprises (SMEs) if they fulfil the criteria summarised in the table below. In addition to the staff headcount ceiling, an enterprise qualifies as an SME if it meets either the turnover ceiling or the balance sheet ceiling, but not necessarily both.

Enterprise category	Headcount	Turnover		Balance sheet total
medium-sized	< 250	≤ 50 million	**or**	≤ 43 million
small	< 50	≤ 10 million		≤ 10 million
micro	< 10	≤ 2 million		≤ 2 million

Primary objectives of social enterprises*

	%
Providing affordable housing	10
Supporting vulnerable children and young people	10
Addressing financial exclusion	13
Protecting the environment	16
Addressing social exclusion	18
Promoting education and literacy	19
Improving health and well-being	22
Supporting vulnerable people	23
Creating employment opportunities	24
Improving a particular community	25

*Respondents could indicate more than one objective

'Fightback Britain' demonstrates that social enterprises actively seek to intervene in the labour market in order to benefit the community where they operate. A clear majority (66%) agreed that they actively recruited staff locally to 'a large extent'. When those who actively recruit locally to some extent are included, this figure jumps to 81%, or four out of every five social enterprises. 'Fightback Britain' also asked whether respondents actively employed people who were disadvantaged in the labour market – people with disabilities, people who are long-term unemployed, offenders and others. A full 25% of their sample agreed that they did this 'to a large extent', a figure that jumps to 56% when those who reported doing this 'to some extent' are included.

For social enterprises in Band One – the most deprived communities – the proportion increases to an astonishing 31% stating that they 'actively employed people who were disadvantaged in the labour market' to 'a large extent'. Very few commercial businesses would employ such people on anything like the scale that is required. In the main, this is because their natural and rightful focus is on building the business. Creating employment is not their objective, let alone their priority, and to make it so would be a distraction. There is also, however, a degree of prejudice against the long-term unemployed among many employers. While I was running Papercycle, I met a businessman whose attitude really shocked me. When I explained my approach to employment, he said to me that he 'would never, in a million years, recruit anyone from a Job Centre – they're obviously lazy'. Since then I have met others with similar views. Although this extreme attitude is relatively unusual, many small-business owners say that they cannot afford to run training programmes for new employees and that candidates need to be skilled enough to do the job on day one.

From two years of unemployment to workshop supervisor

As part of the Future Jobs Fund (FJF) programme, GreenWorks took on Steven in the joinery workshop. This is where we took old desktops, cut them up and re-edged them to make bespoke desks. Steven had been on the dole for two years and had not had a great schooling. He was barely able to complete a full sentence at his interview and struggled with numeracy, but he seemed quite keen. First, we taught him how to operate the edge-banding machine – it is quite a safe machine to use, but you have to concentrate to make sure the edge goes on correctly. After a while, he asked if he could use the dimension saw, which is a very scary tool. We arranged a one-day course for him and the day after he was cutting most of the panels to size. Within a few more weeks, he was helping on the CNC router, a very sophisticated machine that can cut panels to any shape and put holes or cuts in any panel to a pre-determined pattern. This machine was at the heart of our production line.

To be able to operate this machine confidently requires a minimum three-day training course (this does not include programming) which involves some tests along the way. This would have been a daunting prospect for Steven when he started with us but now he completed the course with distinction. Steven became our workshop supervisor, fully responsible for the day-to-day running of the workshop, its production and quality control. The secret to his success was engaged, patient employment.

Finally, the survey shows that at least 71% of social enterprises invest profits in their locality 'to a large extent' and a further 11% invest in the community 'to some extent'. This is a very impressive figure, which demonstrates that money invested in a social enterprise tends to be reinvested in the local area, thereby compounding the benefits.

Further evidence of the job creation tendency of social enterprise is provided by an analysis of employment data by company size. Social enterprises are broadly similar to SMEs in average size by turnover. However, social enterprises seem to employ rather more people for the same turnover.

Social enterprises
20% are start-ups with 0 employees[58]
51% employ 1–9 people
17% employ 10–49 people
12% employ more than 50 people

SMEs
84% employ 1–9 people
14% employ 10–49 people
2.5% employ more than 50 people

This is strong evidence to support the assertion that normal commercial business is less inclined to invest or set up in deprived communities (Band One or Two). The main factors behind those

---

[58] There are likely to be many reasons for the relatively high percentage of social enterprises claiming no employees. Social entrepreneurs commonly work in their community with networks of volunteers, and many, in the start-up phase of the enterprise, do not draw a salary. Also, the contrast between social enterprises and SMEs may not be as stark as it first appears because it is not known how many of the one-person SMEs are actually drawing a salary. More research on this point would be useful.

A Different Perspective

decisions are staff perception of the area (where they work with an existing company that is looking to relocate), a lack of skills locally and the fear of crime and other anti-social behaviour. Social enterprises, on the other hand, take precisely these difficulties as reasons to invest and try to operate their business; they are motivated to tackle the social challenges experienced in these areas. In Band One areas, fully three times as many (proportionately speaking) social enterprises will set up as SMEs. In Band Five zones (the least deprived areas) the ratio is almost reversed, with more than 23% of SMEs locating in these areas as against 9% of social enterprises.

Social enterprises also work hard to include their beneficiaries in their decision-making, which is a vital element of building self-esteem and goes a long way to building both bonding and bridging capital. This type of inclusion can make organisations much more responsive to the needs of their communities. 'Fightback Britain' showed that nearly three-quarters of social enterprises (74%) use this decision-making approach to a greater or lesser extent – a figure that rises to 91% for social enterprises operating in Band One communities.

One of the beneficial by-products of this intense social enterprise activity will be an increased focus on environmental issues. The 'Fightback Britain' survey found that 88% of social enterprises act to minimise their environmental impact, which compares very favourably to small businesses, 44% of whom say they have taken no action whatsoever to do so.[59] Alongside this, 74% of social enterprises monitor their social impact in some way, with 35% reporting that they do this 'to a large extent'.

The analysis in this chapter demonstrates very effectively why a strategy of investment in social enterprise has a greater chance of success in combating worklessness in these deprived areas than anything tried previously. They will undoubtedly create more jobs per pound

---

59 Response to the question: 'Have you changed the way your business operates because of concerns relating to climate change?' in the FSB-ICM 'Voice of Small Business' Annual Survey, 'Report of Key Findings', Federation of Small Businesses (2010).

invested and those jobs are likely to last longer than those created in an SME. Such businesses are also likely to increase levels of social bonding and improve the environment locally. Put simply, if you want a job done properly you go to the specialists. Social entrepreneurs are the specialists in work creation for the least skilled, and they are the specialists in community cohesion and addressing grass-roots problems.

Part 5

My Challenge

Chapter 18

The 1,000 x 1,000 challenge

I offer a bold challenge to the nation – to government (central and local), to business and to the wider community:

> **To create 1,000 new jobs in each of the
> 1,000 most deprived areas of the UK.**

This is a very ambitious national target – it adds up to one million new jobs to be created in the most deprived parts of our country. Judging by past performance, it will be impossible to achieve. If we adopt the same failed approaches we have used in the past, we will fail, and fail expensively.

To meet this challenge and to restore some confidence to our most battered communities we need both a new solution and a new approach. The new solution lies with the thousands of local residents of those areas who want to change things and who have the ideas for making that change. The new approach is to *trust* them and to provide them with consistent, patient support.

Bold thinking is required to address what is at the core of our most pressing social challenges. If we accept the challenge we would be aiming to lift the many millions of workless families off the poverty line and give them new hope. These are people like Bert, Joe, Billy and Keith, who have so much to give but whose personal history has denied them the essential basic and social employability skills to put that potential into action.

The various supply and demand side strategies employed by governments for more than 70 years have failed to resolve the issues faced by those in deep and long-term unemployment.

> The most effective way to break the cycle of deprivation for these people and the communities where they live is to create a large number of new, local, accessible jobs in companies working to a new and more empathetic business model.

> We must create and support new businesses dedicated to providing real jobs for people who are marginalised in the job market.

Patience and perseverance

There have been many calls over the last decade for a more patient form of capital. The logic is that there are many business ideas that need an incubation period before they can take off. They need, therefore, a special kind of persevering, supportive investment to give them the space and time to grow.

All the evidence points to a parallel and urgent requirement for *patient employment*. We require more than jobs and training: we need space in which people from backgrounds of long-term unemployment and multiple deprivation can start to overcome their lack of education, skills and experience.

The need for social entrepreneurs

I have described some of the effects that poor education, low skill levels, imprisonment and long-term unemployment have on people. I have shown that the most effective way to assist someone with such difficulties is to offer them a place of employment that is patient, empathetic, realistic and challenging.

Apart from some honourable exceptions, the private sector is unlikely to create the majority of these jobs. Its priorities are not compatible with the time-consuming and expensive task of patiently helping people from very difficult backgrounds to acquire the basic training and social employability skills that they need to fully participate in the work environment.

For social entrepreneurs such challenges are their priorities. They are willing to accept lower profit margins and lower levels of reward than they could achieve running the same business on commercial lines. They also accept that there will be difficult decisions and ethical challenges in running a social enterprise. They accept all these 'costs' because they are not motivated by material rewards or status.

> In Gandhi's words, social entrepreneurs 'live the change they want to see in the world'.

To create a thousand jobs in a thousand deprived areas we need to give budding and existing social entrepreneurs the tools they need and let them get on with it. In my experience, the relatively small, completely dedicated and energetic local social enterprise that really engages people on the ground is the best vehicle to effect real change. The challenge is therefore: how do you capture enough of this energy to make a real difference to the life of a whole community and help it make a measurable difference to the living standards and aspirations of that community?

Chapter 19

Social Enterprise Zones

The answer is to create Social Enterprise Zones (SEZ). These are designated areas where social enterprises receive incentives to cluster, and where local solutions for local concerns get priority.

SEZ rulebook

Local authorities would be obliged to split down large service contracts to make them more accessible to businesses dedicated to creating local employment for the good of the community. Successful tenders would be those that offer the best value as measured by local benefit (there are tools for measuring this, such as LM3 (Local Multiplier 3) described in the next chapter). Local groups would be empowered to harness local institutional buildings for the community benefit, and any social enterprise operating within a SEZ would qualify to receive employment creation grants. In short, a SEZ would be a space where people are empowered to build their own local solutions.

Each SEZ would actively seek out the countless local people who have answers to some of the problems that they see around them. It would seek to galvanise people to get involved across the whole spectrum of social enterprise, from the youth club run in a businesslike way but dependent on volunteers, to a fully commercial but community-owned recycling business creating employment and jobs for local people.

In this way, we can promote people who know their community well, who can feel and see what needs to be done and can get on and do it. There is no single prescription as to what such areas need. There are only local ideas. If someone thinks that parents would be willing to pay for dance classes for their children, then that is what should happen. If someone else wants to set up a small business employing mainly local people, then they should be encouraged and supported. My mantra is 'go with the energy' – follow the inspiration.

Supporting social enterprise

A key role of a SEZ would be to support aspirant social entrepreneurs and help them gather the skills and the confidence to take on the challenge of creating businesses based not on traditional profit motives, but centred on what is good for their community. Typically, these people have only limited experience of running a business and will need some assistance to set one up. The lack of experience often holds them back.

They ask, 'Can I really run a business?'

'Do I have what it takes to be a businessperson?'

'How do I go about it?'

New social entrepreneurs need practical advice and encouragement to take the plunge and establish a social enterprise in their area. The precise combination of needs will vary from person to person. In my experience, most will need access to start-up funding, guidance about setting up and operating a business and, very importantly, mentoring through the challenges that they will undoubtedly face. As they grow their businesses the nature of the support they require will change. There will be a lot more challenges about leadership, management and staff issues. By creating clusters of social enterprises, we can create a self-help infrastructure that will enable each social entrepreneur to draw on others' experiences to find solutions to their problems as they arise.

Part 6

Where's the Money?

Chapter 20

Reform government spending

One of the key questions in all this is: where does the money come from? Many people will say that a deprived area has very little money. They will ask, how will all these social enterprises survive? How will they earn a living and make profits in an area that has such limited spending power?

The answer is that there is in fact no shortage of money. Enormous sums of money are already being spent in and on these deprived areas. The issue is that too much of the money is in the wrong place or 'leaks' out of the community too quickly. Government and local authorities (and other public bodies) can take a number of measures to redistribute existing monies. They can spend money where it is most needed and ensure that the money has the greatest possible impact on the area.

This section will explore the role of central and local government, and the community itself, in directing and maximising the impact of long-term, focused investments designed to address the scourge of worklessness.

Government priorities

Any successful business sets strategic priorities first, then develops plans and allocates resources according to those priorities. Often incentives are offered to the people in the best position to deliver the required results.

Governments and other big organisations have a wide range of tools that they can use to encourage individuals and businesses (as well as government departments and local authorities) to adopt a particular direction. These range from financial incentives to communication strategies to guide and encourage certain behaviours. Governments regularly tax activities they want to discourage (such as alcohol abuse) and offer tax rebates on activities that they want to encourage (such as pensions investment). They also run campaigns to encourage certain behaviours (such as the Change4Life fitness campaign) or to discourage other behaviours (such as the anti-drink-drive campaigns, which reduced deaths caused by drunk driving from 1,640 in 1979 to around 400 in 2011).

The nation should make worklessness a top (and I mean *top*!) priority. That means government, local authorities and other public bodies must all look at how they can adjust policies, alter programmes and take practical actions to affect this issue in a meaningful way.

It is self-evident to me that businesses should take their share of responsibility for this agenda, as they play an extremely important role in our society. They gain a lot from investments in that society (as employers and as markets) and conversely they suffer when they cannot find the skilled employees they need. A larger pool of labour at every stage in the supply chain and a greater market of potential consumers with new disposable income will benefit business of all sizes.

Area Based Initiatives (ABIs)

With regard to the employment and training aspects of ABIs, authorities should focus their attention on reworking their purchasing polices and redesigning projects to allow small social enterprises to access them. As we will see in the work done by the New Economics Foundation (NEF) cited in chapter 22,[60] the LM3 local multiplier effect is very significant if local people run businesses and in turn spend the money they earn from them in their own area.

Government schemes need focus

Part 3 outlined some of the employment support measures that various governments have introduced. Before moving to innovative ways of raising the finance for this major initiative, we should consider how to reform these current schemes to enable them to create jobs.

I propose three essential reforms:

- Pay the employer directly.

- Pay in proportion to the need.

- Concentrate on the most deprived areas.

The key reform we need to make is the first of the above: to pay qualifying employers and potential employers directly. The intermediary organisations that dominate the management of employment schemes simply add cost and complexity. *They can, and should be removed from the equation.*

With the Future Jobs Fund (FJF) of 2009, we saw that it was possible to operate a large, competitive scheme whereby relatively small social enterprises received payments directly from the

---

60 NEF (New Economics Foundation) is an independent think tank that seeks to improve the quality of life by promoting innovative solutions that challenge mainstream thinking on economic, environmental and social issues.

Department for Work and Pensions. This meant that they received the full amount for each trainee without an intermediary taking a percentage. This covered the costs for the extra supervision involved in working with inexperienced unemployed people. It also meant that each enterprise was responsible for identifying the specific needs of the trainee and was able to cover the costs of any remedial training he or she required. For example at GreenWorks we were able to employ specialist trainers in literacy and numeracy as well vocational NVQs to support our trainees on an individual needs basis.

It should be possible to overcome the cost of making direct payments to employers and also, in the process, to remove the intermediary. It should also be possible to create a system that automatically provides support in proportion to need. Each unemployed person could be assigned an 'employment credit', the size of which would be proportionate to the length of time he/she has been unemployed. It could also reflect the area where the person lives and be graduated according to the recorded level of deprivation there. The credit could be attached to the person's national insurance number or their tax code and would be payable to the employer taking them on. Any employer would be able to see the available 'employment credit' and assess whether that was sufficient to compensate for the lack of skills offered by the candidate. They would get an immediate credit on their employer's national insurance every time they paid that person through the payroll. This would lead to an increase in the resources channelled directly to supporting employment rather than wasting them on the unnecessary administrative 'friction' created by the intermediaries.

The added benefit of this approach is that employers would be able to decide if the people they had taken on required extra assistance or training to enable them to retain their job or get a promotion. The employer is best placed to assess an employee's abilities and training needs. They are also better able to negotiate a good deal on the form and cost of the training package the person actually needs.

Focusing government measures

Employment support should be focused on the geographical areas where worklessness is worst. These would correlate to the lowest bands on the IMD (Index of Multiple Deprivation). There are a number of benefits to this approach.

The schemes would concentrate on those communities that need most help.

A locally based SEZ team would build relationships with willing local employers.

Perhaps most importantly, ministers and politicians would not be distracted by the misleading apparent success rates of more generic nationwide schemes placing people in employment who are already quite close to being job-ready.

Chapter 21

Innovative funding

The government and the EU have determined that putting our rubbish in landfill sites is inherently bad. It is a waste of resources, a waste of good land and potentially highly polluting. It also creates methane, which is a very potent greenhouse gas. The government has therefore adopted a strategy of substantially reducing the volume of rubbish that goes to landfill across the UK. A raft of measures has been introduced to discourage landfill and to encourage more environmentally sustainable methods of waste management such as recycling and reuse.

One of the first fiscal measures John Major's government took in 1996 was the introduction of a tax on landfill waste. The tax is collected on behalf of HMRC by the landfill operators (LOs). It is a relatively easy-to-collect tax as all waste dumped in landfill sites is recorded over a weighbridge.

So far so tedious – this seems to be just another government tax; but here is the innovative part. The government set up a scheme whereby the LOs can get a large (90%) landfill tax rebate on money they donate to specified public environmental projects such as remediating landfill sites, recycling waste, repairing places of worship and other historic buildings, upgrading or creating public amenities and conserving wildlife.[61] What makes the scheme even better is that many LOs will only pay their 90% to the projects if those schemes raise the first 10%. In this way charities such as the RSPB have run very successful 'you give £1 and we get £10' fundraising schemes which really encourage third parties to donate.

The results are impressive: between 1996 and 2011 more than £1 billion has been donated to 'Environmental Bodies' (EBs) to spend on the projects they have developed. So far, 25,000 public parks and other amenities have been improved; more than 5,000 churches and other historic sites have been repaired; and more than 2,000 waste reduction, recycling and land remediation schemes have been funded.

Total spent on the objects of the Landfill Communities Fund

The remediation of land (Object A)	£19.4m
The prevention of pollution (Object B)	£2m
The reduction of waste (Object C)	£247.7m
The recycling of waste (Object CC)	£4.7m
Public parks and public amenities (Object D)	£571m
Biodiversity conservation (Object DA)	£43m
The restoration of places of worship and historic buildings (Object E)	£67.8m
The provision of services to other environmental bodies (Object J)	£2.3m

Here we have a superb example of an innovative tax that increases

---

61 The Landfill Communities Fund (LCF) enables operators of landfill sites to contribute money to enrolled Environmental Bodies (EBs) to carry out projects that meet environmental objectives contained in the Landfill Tax Regulations. Landfill operators (LOs) can contribute up to 6.2% of their landfill tax liability to EBs, and reclaim 90% of this contribution as a tax credit. They may bear the remaining 10% themselves, or an independent third party can make up this 10% difference to the LO.

the costs to business of engaging in an environmentally undesirable activity (landfill) and puts a fair proportion of that tax towards helping community projects across the country. Because the LOs are at the heart of the system, they have an opportunity to raise their profile in a positive way with the community, which makes them very willing to (a) take part in the scheme and (b) bear the costs of administering it.

The potential benefits are substantially understated. As a local councillor between 1998 and 2002, I sat on the panel for the Western Riverside Environment Fund (WREF),[62] which distributed landfill tax revenues to local projects. The principal condition of funding was that WREF was a part-funder and that the project had to raise a substantial proportion ('match funding' in the parlance) of the required investment from other sources. In most cases, the WREF investment amounted to around 20% of the project costs.

The effect of this policy was that our funding acted as a magnet for projects to attract four to five times more. Projects were able to attract money from Europe as well as funds from philanthropic sources, local authority grants and various government departments. Many carried out local fund-raising as well.

Redundancy levy

I am proposing that we adopt a similar approach to the big issue of our time – worklessness. In such a scenario, redundancy would stand in the same relationship to employment as landfill currently stands to recycling. Redundancy is the societal 'bad' thing that we would like to prevent and employment for our most marginalised people is the social good we wish to promote. Therefore, we should

---

62 This panel managed the process of spending landfill tax credits generated from the waste landfilled by the four boroughs of Lambeth, Wandsworth, Kensington & Chelsea and Hammersmith & Fulham (the constituent boroughs of the Western Riverside Waste Authority).

Where's the Money?

place a levy on redundancy payments. We could then offer a tax rebate, similar to the landfill tax rebate, on a significant proportion of that 'redundancy levy' where the money is donated to job creation schemes in deprived areas nearby.

Overcoming the difficulties

No doubt, there will be several objections to such a scheme. Let us examine the most obvious ones:

- **It will be unfair to reduce the tax-free sum received by those made redundant at a time when they need it the most.**

I am not in any way advocating a reduction in the tax-free payments received by employees made redundant. If necessary, the legislation introducing the levy should specify that redundancy benefits could not be affected by the proposed levy.

- **Businesses will not be able to afford such a levy at a time of distress.**

Clearly, this is a very real consideration and one with which I can empathise. I have personally experienced very difficult trading circumstances and have several times needed to make people redundant. I would not want in any way to endanger the survival of a business going through difficult times. For this reason, I am *not* proposing that the levy should be punitive. The optimum size of the levy is debatable but £1,000 per person, irrespective of time served or salary package, would be a good starting point for research and assessment. It may also be appropriate to exclude small businesses with fewer than 15 employees from the levy.

- **We need to keep flexibility in the labour market and leave employers free to hire and fire.**

A levy could increase genuine flexibility of employment. Currently, redundancy is the most straightforward route for businesses to take to reduce costs and because of that, other solutions are often not properly considered. If the levy made employers think a bit more creatively about whether people needed to leave the business, that would be a good thing in the current economic situation. Job shares, part-time contracts and pay cuts are all options. There is often a myriad of alternative solutions that could replace the standard one of making people redundant.

The GreenWorks example

In 2010, GreenWorks was seeking significant reductions in its administration costs. The volume of business had declined and we had streamlined some of the processes, so we did not need so many staff. We called the two administrators, Andrea and Terry, into a meeting and explained that we were creating a new 'super' administrator position combining their roles. This would mean that there would only be one administrator. We set out the criteria for the new post and both of them were invited to apply for the job. We added that we would be very interested in hearing any ideas that they might have about how to reduce our administration costs but we felt that the super administrator idea was the most likely to succeed.

We knew both of them wanted full-time work and we really thought that in the end we would have to make a very tough choice between them. Both of them had been with GreenWorks for several years and each offered different skills and attributes to the business.

After a week or so of consultation and several conversations with our excellent Human Resources Manager, Andrea and Terry put forward an amazing proposition. They had agreed to share the job and both go part-time. At first, I was very sceptical, but as we went through the details, I began to realise that the solution offered a number of benefits to GreenWorks. We would lose none of the IT experience and client knowledge that Andrea and Terry had built up between them. We would benefit from improved sickness and holiday cover and we would not have to pay out any redundancy pay. Lastly, and for me very importantly, we were able to live up to our reputation of being a good employer and genuinely listening to our staff.

We put the job-share scheme into place immediately and it worked extremely well.

- **Why should businesses from one area be obliged to support work creation schemes in another area?**

Employers operating in a Band One area would be able to invest the rebated amounts into their own area. Other organisations working in less deprived areas would be obliged to invest in schemes in a nearby Band One area. This is justified by the sheer scale of the problem and the benefits that will accrue to all if we can address it. Helping the long-term unemployed to get work is by any measure a very positive thing for the whole of society.

- **Why should the levy apply equally to all staff facing redundancy irrespective of length of service or salary package?**

Applying the levy as a flat rate for all, including those with the shortest service or who are the lowest paid, would incentivise the retention of this very vulnerable group of employees. In this way, the policy would encourage greater job security for those who need it the most.

Overall, if such a levy made a few employers think again about making staff redundant, that would be a good thing.

Labour Force Survey (LFS)

Redundancies 1995–2012

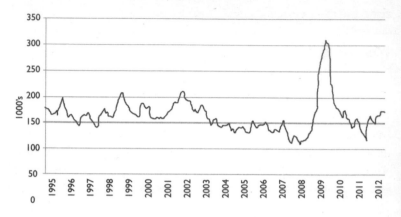

The Labour Force Survey (LFS) has recorded data on redundancies since 1995. Over that period an average of 164,000 people have been made redundant every quarter. This equates to more than 650,000 people laid off per year. What is most striking about this graph is that, apart from the terrible peak in the immediate aftermath of the collapse of Lehman Bros in September 2008, the level of redundancies stays remarkably consistent. No matter where we are in the economic cycle, large numbers of people are made redundant every year. When one considers the wider circle of families and friends who are affected when someone is made redundant, these numbers clearly represent a lot of pain and anguish for millions of people. The point I am making here, though, is that the consistency of the numbers makes them a very plausible source of finance. At a rate of £1,000 per person, the total raised by the redundancy levy would be £650 million per year. If, for instance, 50% of that was able to attract a 90% levy discount when it was directed to schemes supporting job creation in deprived areas, that would amount to £292.5 million per annum.

Where's the Money?

The consistency of the redundancy data through good years and bad suggests that one of the benefits of a redundancy levy is that it will provide the long-term funding to underpin the patient, long-term entrepreneurial business model.

Match funding

The redundancy levy would provide the bedrock of investment for programmes to tackle long-term and embedded worklessness. More importantly, it would act as a catalyst for other investment aimed at addressing this issue. For example, it would be eligible as match funding for EU programmes aimed at addressing structural social and development issues in deprived areas. Private philanthropic trusts would be very interested in supporting such projects as well. When combined with various other local and central government funding and support programmes it would be possible to create a really effective annual investment fund of about £1 billion for investing in creating businesses in the most deprived areas.

Chapter 22

Locking in local money

As well as drawing money from outside an area, it is possible to make much better use of the money already spent within it.

There are two main sources of money in a given area: that spent on local services by public authorities (the council, emergency services, health service and so on), and the money spent by the residents in the community. Even in the most deprived areas, these two sources amount to quite substantial sums. Unfortunately, a lot of the money spent by public bodies on providing services does not benefit the local community. Too much of it disappears into companies and institutions based outside the area.

Public authority services

Let us first look at public authority spending. The biggest institutions in many deprived areas are public bodies such as the NHS, the police and the local council. With a more creative and entrepreneurial approach, these public bodies could issue contracts for a range of services to local firms and social enterprises. Local businesses could provide, for example, local bus services, office cleaning, security, taxis, flowers, porterage, grounds maintenance and window cleaning. This will require some new ways of thinking by the authorities in terms of putting contracts out to tender. The benefits in health, security and well-being for the people these authorities serve should spur them to overcome the obvious bureaucratic obstacles.

These 'physical' services are very labour-intensive and stand in an organic relationship with the expectations and skill levels of the local community. They naturally lend themselves to delivery by local firms employing local people.

The concept of local employment would bring other benefits. As an example, it could be an effective way of resolving the increasingly large social welfare dilemmas facing this country. The NHS and local authority social services departments are facing the care demands of an ever-increasing number of elderly and other infirm people. There is general agreement that caring for such people is best done at home; this way they can maintain contact with friends and neighbours. It is also a more cost-effective solution than admitting people to hospital. Currently home visit services are contracted out by health authorities to firms covering very wide geographical areas. A number of concerns typically expressed about this sort of service range from the short amount of time spent with each person to the impersonal nature of the service. These concerns could be addressed in large measure by parcelling up smaller, geographically focused service contracts for locally run small businesses or social enterprises. Such an approach would see an increase in the employment of local people, a reduction in journey time between visits and hopefully an increase in familiarity with the staff for the infirm person.

So far, we have explored the potential for public authorities to utilise their spending power in ways that would assist their local community. Public authorities could go even further. As virtually permanent fixtures in the area, they have assets that can be put to use for the benefit of the local community. In an area where property ownership is limited, permanence assumes greater importance.

Look at the example of Cleveland, Ohio in the United States. It is an extremely depressed area, whose population has shrunk in a few decades from 1 million to around 386,000 souls. The local hospitals there are the biggest employers in the area. They are also the most permanent 'anchor' institutions in the community – they are extremely unlikely to leave Cleveland. Between them and the university, they spend more than $3 billion a year on supplies. Paradoxically these very wealthy institutions are located at the heart of an area of Cleveland where 40% of the population live below the poverty line. Only recently, though, did they realise that they have a vested interest in the well-being of the local community.

When Ted Howard of the Evergreen Cooperative pointed out the huge deprivation that existed on their doorstep and that their procurement offered a key to improving the area, the hospitals started to work together. Among many compatible initiatives, Ted Howard demonstrated that the hospital roofs were the ideal place to install solar panels. The hospitals have commissioned a local worker-owned cooperative, Ohio Cooperative Solar (OCS), to install and maintain an array of solar panels. OCS owns the panels and has full responsibility for them. It then sells the energy generated at an agreed price to the hospitals. In this way, the investment produces a steady income stream for the cooperative, allowing it to expand its installation and engineering business and employ more local people. The traditional model of purchasing electricity from large power suppliers operating large, capital-intensive power stations creates very little employment, and all of the money the institutions spend on electricity used to leave the community, bringing it no benefit. The Cleveland model shows how providing a capital-intensive service at a local level can create local benefits and employment.

Could this model be extended to other essential services requiring heavy capital investment? One candidate would be waste and resource management. Until recently, waste was viewed as something to dispose of as quickly and cleanly as possible and has had

Where's the Money?

very negative connotations. However, as resource consumption grows and competition for resources increases, people are viewing waste as a valuable source of materials. Traditionally, authorities and large businesses have contracted companies to remove their waste as cleanly and quickly as possible. This now means that those, typically remote, companies have control of what we increasingly view as potentially valuable resources. The Cleveland model suggests that a new approach might be possible: one that allows the local community to extract the resource value from its own waste.

Managing waste as a resource and increasing the amount recycled could create an extra 70,000 jobs across the UK.[63] Recycling is labour-intensive – it requires a lot of people to collect, grade and sell the materials. Even more jobs can be created by reusing products (as in Cybercycle, Renew and GreenWorks), and these jobs will tend to be more skilled. A recent Environment Protection Agency (EPA) report from the USA suggests that for every 10,000 tonnes of materials, incinerating creates one job; landfilling creates six jobs; recycling creates 36 jobs; and reuse of these same materials can create between 28 and 296 jobs.[64]

The New Economics Foundation (NEF) has done an extraordinary amount of work measuring the financial impact of how various services are tendered and commissioned. They have identified significant differences in the amounts of money that each approach retains in the locality.

Value of government spending could be doubled by buying local

When they launched their report, 'The Money Trail', in April 2003, NEF stated that a 'focus on supply chain in disadvantaged areas will create more jobs and regeneration. Communities, business and government can increase, even double, the amount of money flowing

---

63 Friends of the Earth report, 'More Jobs Less Waste', September 2010.

64 'Waste to Wealth: Recycling Means Business' by the Institute for Local Self Reliance, commissioned by the US Environmental Protection Agency.

into and being retained in the local economy of disadvantaged urban and rural areas by fostering links in the local business supply chain. This is a vital strategy in regenerating such areas and improving the quality of life for people living there.

'The Money Trail' outlines, in step-by-step accessible terms, how to use a tool called Local Multiplier 3 (LM3). Pilot studies of the LM3 tool have found that:

- government spending on a local construction firm benefited the local economy nearly twice as much as spending on a non-local firm;

- an organic farm's income generated twice as much money for the local economy as a supermarket's income in the same area; and

- local cash points are vital to the survival of high streets because people spend between half and two-thirds of their withdrawal immediately in the local area.

Justin Sacks, manager of NEF's LM3 programme, said: 'The implications for local and national government of the findings thus far are huge. Using smart, local spending strategies, which "The Money Trail" can help to identify, it is possible to help money stick where it's targeted, turning around the economies of areas with few jobs and economic opportunities.'

Research in Northumberland

Northumberland County Council has developed this concept and they reported a very significant impact after using this LM3. In March 2005 NEF issued a press release entitled 'Buying local worth 400 per cent more'. It read,

Local authorities could increase the amount of money circulating in their area by 400 per cent by examining how they spend their money, and fostering links with local suppliers. Northumberland County Council used NEF's Local Multiplier 3 (LM3) methodology to track the value of its local spending, to measure its impact – and how that impact could be increased. Northumberland's research found that:

• In addition to the initial contracts, local suppliers in Northumberland re-spent on average 76 per cent of their income from contracts with local people and businesses, while suppliers from outside Northumberland spent only 36 per cent in the area.

• This means that every £1 spent with a local supplier is worth £1.76 to the local economy, and only 36 pence if it is spent out of the area. That makes £1 spent locally worth almost 400 per cent more.

• A 10 per cent increase in the proportion of the council's annual procurement spent locally would mean £34 million extra circulating in the local economy each year.

• If councils across the UK made a 10 per cent increase in using local businesses, it could mean an additional £5.6 billion re-circulating in local economies across the UK. This is a powerful and vital tool for local authorities who need to target the benefits of spending on disadvantaged areas.

• The result of the food contract tendering process was a fivefold increase in local suppliers' expressions of interest, which resulted in four of seven product categories (meat, milk, bread, fruit and vegetables) being awarded to local suppliers – almost half the value of the county's £3 million food procurement budget.

• Breaking a contract into lots, as Northumberland did, allows local suppliers to enter the tendering process, and gives the contracting organisation a more customer-focused and competitive service overall. Northumberland found that developing stronger links with local suppliers also strengthened community spirit – the 'social glue' that holds communities together and plays an essential role in regeneration. There is more administrative work involved, but council officers found that this was repaid by the quantity and quality of the tenders received, and the community links developed.

Residents' spending

The second great area of spend in a community is the money that individual residents spend on goods and services of their choice. Once again, NEF found that this money could be spent more effectively and be locked into the community better if it was spent with locally owned and run shops and providers.

One study on spending on take-away food in a housing estate illustrates how it works. Marsh Farm is a large housing estate in Luton, Bedfordshire, which mainly consists of council and social housing. The residents of the estate spend more than £1 million per year on take-away food. All the take-away shops are part of national chains, and while these take-aways employ some local people, the majority of the revenue going through these shops goes directly to the chains' headquarters. Less than 20% of the money spent in these take-aways sticks in Marsh Farm. The obvious conclusion is to develop locally owned take-aways. Where local people own the shops, NEF have demonstrated that significantly more money stays in the local community. In addition to employing local people, the local owners purchase products and services through the local supply chain and of course spend some of their own earnings locally. The net result is that the amount of money sticking in the community is estimated to rise to between 50 and 70%.

The take-away example leads one to think about groceries in general. In so many very deprived areas access to fresh food is limited, and the food itself is expensive and of poor quality. This leads to disproportionate spending on take-away food, with the loss of revenue we have seen above and, of course, the associated health issues. If local people could be encouraged to set up grocery stores or to grow food locally on allotments for local sale, not only would they lock in more revenue to the area but the health of the residents would improve as well.

Another way of locking money into an area and plugging the leaks that NEF identifies is to adopt a local, complementary currency. This is a system of money that operates alongside the standard national currency. It is used in the same way as money in any shop that accepts it in a designated area. A study of the West Michigan Economy in the US concluded that if residents of the area were to redirect 10% of their total spending from chains to locally owned businesses, the result would be $140 million in new economic activity for the region, including 1,600 new jobs.

Local currencies

The **Brixton Pound (B£)** is the UK's first local currency in an urban area and Brixton is the fourth place to have its own currency, following the Totnes Pound in Devon, the Lewes Pound in Sussex and the Stroud Pound in Gloucestershire. It is a complementary currency, working alongside (not replacing) pounds sterling, for use by independent local shops and traders.

A government press release states:

> The benefits of local shopping have been documented by studies in the UK and US. On average supermarkets and other large chains spend just 10–12 pence in every pound in the local community (New Economics Foundation, 2002). The rest 'leaks out' to shareholders, international suppliers and national support and distribution services. In contrast, small independent shops are more likely to employ local firms for these services and spend any profits locally.
>
> Small businesses account for the majority of UK private sector jobs: 59.2% in 2007, around 13.5 million jobs overall.* However, figures from the Federation of Small

Businesses show dramatic decline in local shops and services across the UK, with 2,000 local shops closing each year and 39 pubs closing each week. During recession, supporting local businesses is particularly vital and the Brixton Pound is a practical way for local people to vote with their wallets for a strong and diverse Brixton economy.

* Department for Business, Enterprise and Regulatory Reform statistical press release, 30 July 2008.

Corporate supply chain

In 1975, E. F. Schumacher asked a fundamental question in his extraordinary book, *Small is Beautiful*. Why can't business work profitably to solve the real issues that humans want solved, such as employment, hunger, housing, clean water, and so on? For the last 35-plus years that question seems to have lain dormant, but that attitude is now starting to change.

In their seminal work 'Creating Shared Value'[65] Michael E. Porter and Mark R. Kramer suggest that, 'Not all profit is equal. Profits involving a social purpose represent a higher form of capitalism, one that creates a positive cycle of company and community prosperity.'

In their paper, they outline three ways in which corporations can harness their 'full potential to meet society's broader challenges'. They are:

- reconceiving products and markets;

- redefining productivity in the value chain; and

- enabling local cluster development.

Reconceiving products and markets

Companies should take a long look at 'Creating Shared Value' and closely examine what markets they are in, where the greatest *real* need

65 'Creating Shared Value', Michael E. Porter and Mark R. Kramer, *Harvard Business Review*, January 2011.

is and how they can deliver profitable services to address that need. Porter and Kramer offer a range of examples on how to 'reconceive the market'. They ask companies to look a bit harder at their markets. They encourage them to ask a more fundamental question – not what can we sell them, but rather what do they want, or indeed, what do they need. They discuss the fact that major food companies are (finally) looking at improving the nutritional value of their food rather than just its attractiveness. They demonstrate the example of Vodafone helping millions of small farmers in Kenya to trade and bank very quickly and cheaply through their mobile phones, and they cite General Electric's well-known Ecoimagination scheme.

Redefining productivity in the value chain

The second aspect of Porter and Kramer's approach in this paper is to look hard at the value chain. They bemoan the constant search for the next low-cost production base as it places incredible stress on the supply chain. They point out that suppliers whose margins are constantly under pressure cannot remain productive or sustain output over the long term. Moreover, they cannot improve the quality of their output.

If, however, a company can work with such suppliers and assist them with investment, better technology and better management, they can improve the quality and certainty of supply. In their example of Nespresso, they show that the close involvement of the company with the small growers on which it depends for its supply of coffee beans brought improved yields, better quality beans and a reduction in the environmental impact on the soil. Both parties won in this example of Creating Shared Value.

Porter and Kramer go on to develop the point further by emphasising the benefits of using local suppliers: 'Capable local suppliers help firms avoid these costs and reduce cycle time, increase flexibility, foster faster learning and enable innovation …' When firms buy locally, their suppliers grow stronger, increase their profits, hire more people and pay better wages; all of which benefits other businesses in the community.

Enabling local cluster development

Finally, Porter and Kramer illustrate the idea of 'Enabling local cluster development'. They point out that, 'Clusters are prominent in all successful and growing regional economies and play a crucial role in driving productivity, innovation and competitiveness.' They also point out the obvious converse that costs will increase 'when clusters do not operate effectively or are constrained in some way'. In their words, 'deficiencies in the framework conditions surrounding the cluster also create internal costs for firms'. Poor public education imposes productivity and remedial training costs. Poor transportation infrastructure drives up the costs of logistics. Gender or racial discrimination reduces the pool of capable employees. Poverty limits the demand for products and leads to environmental degradation, unhealthy workers and high security costs. They go on to say, 'as companies have increasingly become disconnected from their communities, however, their influence in solving these problems has waned even as their costs have grown'.

They recommend that companies look hard at the deficiencies in their area of operations, whether they be in training, logistics or somewhere else. They should then actively seek partners from across the spectrum of public, private and third sector providers to collaborate with them to address these shortcomings.

The local supply chain

At first glance, it would seem that the three approaches outlined by Porter and Kramer inherently address the issue of the supply chain. However, we should focus closely on the supply chain as the best source of long-term sustainable funding. The issue of worklessness will prove impervious to our efforts otherwise.

All organisations have to buy a wide range of goods and services to sustain themselves. These range from materials or products that firms use directly in manufacturing their own products, to services or materials that they use to support their workforce. They purchase these goods from a range of companies that supply specialist services to them. In the jargon this is called the supply chain: the network of smaller companies providing the raw materials, engineering services, cleaning, toilet paper, catering services and so on that the organisation needs to maintain its operation and provide for the staff. Because the supply chain is essential to the running of the organisation, spending here is clearly more sustainable. Moreover, being part of the supply chain requires the vital business disciplines that engender real engagement in employment and skills among people from low-skilled, long-term unemployed backgrounds.

The process will also work both ways. There is evidence that companies adopting such a proactive stance on social procurement gain a far better understanding of the issues involved and the solutions needed. As a result of their company's involvement, staff are more willing to engage in volunteering and other related works. In turn, this boosts morale and improves staff retention rates. This is a great example of Porter and Kramer's assertion that this sort of work should be at the heart of a company's activities and not at the periphery.

To that end, all corporations, local authorities and central government departments should set targets for procuring goods and services from locally run companies that are actively investing in the sort of long-term employment and training approaches necessary to break the cycle of low skills and dependence. The size of the target would vary depending on the nature of the organisation and the nature of its supply chain. As a starting point, I would advocate at least 5% of supply chain procurement contracts be placed with such firms. By way of comparison, the hospitals in Cleveland that I referred to earlier are looking to exceed 25% local spend in the next few years.

Furthermore, large organisations should commit to accepting that such suppliers, because they are employing and training 'hard to reach' people, have inherently higher costs. This should be reflected in the corporation accepting a reasonable price premium on these services in the first instance. They should then commit to working with the supplier in a proactive way to enable them to reduce their costs over time *whilst still achieving the social outcomes*. This support could take the form of pro bono managerial, legal and accounting advice. Small businesses would also benefit from technology sharing, marketing support and market development and networking opportunities with other like-minded procurers.

Non-financial contributions

There are other resources that large institutions could provide which would be very useful to local social enterprises. For instance, could they release spare office space to a local social enterprise? Could school classrooms or playgrounds be used after hours or during holidays? Could the corporate office offer some of its meeting rooms to community groups?

A local authority can of course also take a proactive role in supporting business development. When Gateshead Metropolitan Borough Council (GMBC) contracted with me to set up what became Renew North East they clearly wanted to get involved in whatever way they could. Their support and active involvement was extremely useful in paving the way for the new business. They were able to broker meetings with the major funding organisations in the area as well as with local businesses. The council was then keen to take the involvement to the next logical step and take a seat on the board. They realised that being on the board would enable them to understand the issues that Renew faced and assist it to overcome them. Moreover, they wanted to ensure that Renew provided the maximum possible benefit for the local community. In order to comply with the restrictions placed on councils in the Local Government and Housing Act 1989, we formed a board of seven directors. Six were local people from a variety of backgrounds and the council took up the seventh position. Having a GMBC representative on the board proved to be a very useful asset throughout the period of my involvement with the company. We were at different times able to access important employee management advice, health and safety guidance, alerts about potential funding and an immeasurable amount of administrative and background support from some very committed officers in the Local Initiatives Team.

External trade

Many social enterprises will create and supply services to buyers from outside the area, thereby bringing new money into the locality. At GreenWorks very little of its revenue came from within the London Borough of Brent, which is a very deprived borough in the northwest of London. Large corporate organisations in the City and West End commissioned the service, which effectively acted as a redistributive mechanism to translate money earned in the City into jobs and revenue in Brent. It is a caricature of social enterprises that they are small set-ups providing local services at tight margins. It is true that there are many in that category, but there are many other examples of social enterprises that have the capacity to take on large contracts with major organisations. Contracts with well-known brands or foreign firms have a remarkable psychological and motivational impact on staff, and in particular on staff from deprived backgrounds.

Do you remember Keith? He was the young man who introduced his brother Jake to our company when he came out of prison. Keith was having quite a bad time of it. He was living with his dad, who had a violent criminal background, and Keith was steadily being drawn into this world. His dad encouraged Keith to participate in crime and when he refused became extremely abusive. Keith wanted a job so that he could get away from the house and the surrounding criminal fraternity. Ultimately, he wanted to save enough money to move out altogether.

After a while working with Papercycle he became the forklift driver. He was a bright kid and that shone through, even though his education had clearly been a very hit-and-miss affair. As the forklift driver, he did a good job and he was visibly growing in confidence as a person.

I had not realised quite how much the job meant to him until the day we shipped a load to Holland. This was the first time we had ever exported anything. It was crucial to get a perfect 22 tonnes on the truck to get the best value out of the deal, but without going over the weight limit for the truck. Keith was brilliant. He carefully but quickly assessed each bale of paper and got to within 20 kilograms of the 22-tonne (22,000-kilogram) limit. I was delighted when the load left the yard and told him so immediately.

The real significance dawned on me the next day, though. I walked out of the warehouse as Keith was on his smoke break and I overheard him talking to a mechanic from the workshop next door. As I passed, he took a deep tug on his fag and said in a grave and thoughtful tone, 'So yeah, we're exporting to Holland now.'

I could hear the pride resonating in his voice. I reflected later on how the idea of 'exporting to Holland' had increased his self-respect and boosted his self-confidence.

Summary

The problem of worklessness is deeply entrenched. It cannot be solved by government alone. Nor will the efforts of local people be enough to make a sustainable difference: large business needs to make its contribution too. However, in the same way as I've argued for a more focused contribution by government, so too we require more application by business. We do not want CSR schemes that serve some PR agenda – we want real contracts. If corporations used just a fraction of their buying power to support businesses based in deprived areas or SEZs they would have a dramatic, positive impact on that community.

Conclusion

We need to acknowledge long-term unemployment and worklessness as the major, unmentioned, but avoidable social issue of our time. Worklessness marks millions more peoples' lives than is commonly recognised. It is also far more debilitating in its effects than most people understand.

The issue of worklessness is unmentioned because the problem is hidden from view in concentrated areas where most people do not venture. It is also unmentioned because we have a culture that seems to believe that unemployment is the fault of the unemployed. How else could we blame individuals for not getting a job when there are 6.5 million people chasing less than half a million vacancies?

But worklessness is avoidable. We can do something about it: we can create meaningful and useful work for these people. To do so, though, we must first of all make job creation our true priority. And then, we must take effective action to do something that actually works. We need to do this for the sake of our economy but also because I believe it is our *moral* duty to redress a terrible inequity.

Economically the argument is very straightforward. If we get more people into work, we will increase our GDP. We will also increase our tax base, reduce the cost of benefits, improve the health of our people and probably reduce crime rates.

Morally? Well, we know that the young people who struggled to find work in the eighties recession have suffered reduced earnings and more fragmented work patterns for their whole lives. Indeed, we use that argument quite rightly to demand urgent action to address youth unemployment now so that we can avoid creating another class of indelibly scarred individuals.

I think we should equally argue for those people whom our education system neglected in previous decades. Surely, we owe something to those children, now adults, who went through an education system that sent in excess of 50% of its charges to secondary school unable to read functionally, *and* that failed that same 50% throughout secondary school and left them with virtually no qualifications. They were let down then, but that surely should not mean that we condemn them to a life of fragmented employment, poverty and early death?

In addition to the moral case for helping those whose education we neglected we should consider the powerful effect they have on today's young people as role models. If we are to help the majority of our young people to find work, we have to set the right example and change the aura of defeatism that exists in so many communities.

There is also a very pragmatic reason why we should put real effort into helping these people. Unequal societies suffer from much higher levels of stress and insecurity across *all* strata of society. With 6.5 million workless people in our society, inequality is growing wider every day, and every one of us feels the effects.

The case for a fresh approach

Successive governments have expended enormous amounts of money on trying to relieve unemployment. Unfortunately, a considerable proportion of that money has been misdirected or poorly managed. As a result, most of it has failed to reach the people most difficult to employ, who need the most help.

We need a new approach to this problem. We must make tackling worklessness a top priority. Let us take up the challenge of creating 1,000 jobs in each of the 1,000 most deprived communities in our country. Let us commit to making the legislative and fiscal changes needed to make that target achievable. Let us also agree to support the people who really *want* to change things: to invest time and money recruiting, supporting and developing social entrepreneurs from within the communities themselves, and empower them to create jobs.

Social entrepreneurs

I have shown that individuals experiencing unemployment can have very complex and challenging issues to deal with before they can progress, but, paradoxically, they will tackle those issues best when they have a job. Creating jobs for such people is a labour of love and a fantastic challenge. Only those motivated from the start to do this will succeed in meeting the challenge. If you want something done properly you go to the experts, and social entrepreneurs are the experts in creating jobs in deprived areas.

To enable social entrepreneurs to operate effectively in deprived areas and to bring about the change and the regeneration we want to see, we need to rewrite the rulebook. New rules are required to make it possible for small local social enterprises to thrive in these depressed areas; new rules are required to oversee the relationship between communities and the authorities that serve them; new rules are required for the way we regard people whom the system has neglected; and finally, new rules are needed for the approach we take to relieving worklessness. We need rules that encourage the creation of jobs that sit 'in some organic relationship' with the skills and expectations of the community where they are created.

Social Enterprise Zones

We need to establish Social Enterprise Zones (SEZ) as places that embody the new rulebook. Local authorities (councils, health and police authorities) would be obliged to tender locally and to decide winning tenders on the basis of the local benefit a contractor will bring (using assessment tools such as LM3). They would also be encouraged to create local benefit from their fixed assets.

SEZs would be empowered to create incentives for social enterprises (and other businesses wanting to contribute to the local economy and employ local people) to locate within them. Unemployed people living in SEZs would be eligible for higher rates of employment assistance to enable them to find a job.

The funding to create SEZs would come from two sources. First, we must reengineer the Work Programme so that it directly supports the businesses that create new jobs. The intermediaries that currently capture the lion's share of the Work Programme should be excluded. Second, new start-up funding could be generated from a redundancy levy on firms making people redundant. The majority of funds raised by the levy should be focused on creating jobs in the SEZs and other designated areas of high unemployment.

The government should redouble its efforts to include SMEs (small and medium enterprises) in its supply chain and, in particular, to encourage firms based in Social Enterprise Zones. As part of that effort, it should encourage larger companies to work with social enterprises and other firms located in designated unemployment hot spots and SEZs.

Planting the seeds

We have seen that a tremendous passion for changing society does exist and that there are many practical ways of harnessing that passion. We have seen there is plenty of money to back up that passion if we rethink how and where we spend it. Apart from the support of government, what is missing? What do we need to do to bring together those people, that passion and that money to bring substantive change to areas suffering with the sorts of apparently deep and intractable problems identified throughout this book?

Each SEZ will require its very own Elzéard Bouffier – a hard-working, patient, resourceful and open-minded person who will plant and nurture as many social entrepreneurial seeds as it takes to bring these deprived areas to life. I believe that if we plant social enterprises in sufficient numbers they can provide the shade for other new businesses to operate in. If we plant enough of them, in a cluster, we will see a genuine blossoming of communities that would otherwise continue to breed despair and lethargy.

These Elzéards will face a considerable number of trials. They will have to challenge the tired thinking that has failed our deprived areas for so long. They will have to challenge out-of-date ideas of tendering ever larger contracts. They will have to challenge the appalling prejudice that bedevils the long-term unemployed and the areas where they live.

They will, though, have two great allies in this endeavour: the local communities with all their latent talent, creativity and resourcefulness, and the social entrepreneurs who believe that good business has a moral purpose and that this can change people's lives.

DATE AND LOCATION	COLIN'S VENTURES
Early 1990s, Brixton, London **Proprietor of my first social enterprise!**	**Papercycle** I started with £300, collecting paper from businesses for recycling.
Mid-1990s, **Founder**	**3Re** I set up this consultancy to advise clients on how to be more sustainable.
1998–2002, Gateshead **Lead consultant and Chair**	**Renew North East** My biggest and most ambitious consulting project.
1998–2002, Lambeth, London **Local councillor**	**Lambeth Borough Council**
2001–2004, Franchises in Leeds, Newham and Woolwich **CEO**	**Renew Trust** Comet asked me to expand the Renew idea nationally.
2000–2001, Brixton and Camberwell, London **MD**	**Cybercycle** I managed this small social enterprise.

Timeline

HOW AND WHY?	WHAT DID I LEARN?
Within a year or two, we became the first business to collect anything that was recyclable on one van, i.e. paper and cardboard, cans, plastic cups (complete with dregs of sugar and tea!) and printer cartridges. At its height, I employed 15 people, all of whom had previously been unemployed.	I learned my first lessons about marketing: don't restrict your future business by the choice of business name and don't rely on markets that you cannot influence.
I developed a new hands-on waste audit service that measured a firm's waste.	You can offer a new service to an existing market.
Gateshead council asked me to set up a new social enterprise to train local young unemployed people to repair and refurbish second-hand cookers, washing machines and fridges. This business still provides useful skills and work training to people on the margins.	Dynamic social enterprise + support of a local authority = a winning formula for jobs.
Here I met many charities, schools and other social enterprises working hard, with limited resources, to help people who were really struggling.	Local authorities have the potential to really improve lives and benefit communities.
Initially this worked really well. Working with a range of social enterprises and with Remploy, we set up several projects. Unfortunately, Renew Trust lost its funding support and was unable to continue.	Don't become dependent on one organisation!
Based in a run-down Brixton housing estate, the project attracted scores of young unemployed people who not only learnt to fix computers, but also became interested in learning other skills.	Even the least educated person can pick up complex technical skills.

DATE AND LOCATION	COLIN'S VENTURES
2000–2012, Woolwich and Wembley, London, with franchises in Wolverhampton, Paisley, Liverpool, Portsmouth and Bristol **Founder and CEO**	**GreenWorks** In 2000, I had a blinding flash of inspiration on a train outside Darlington.
2006–present **Witness**	**School for Social Entrepreneurs**
2010–present **Chair**	**London Community Resource Network**
2011–present **Founder and CEO**	**Tree Shepherd** Can I use my experience to create jobs where they are really needed?

HOW AND WHY?	WHAT DID I LEARN?
Starting out with around £500, I began collecting office furniture. My big break came when HSBC moved to Canary Wharf – and had to dispose of 3,500 tonnes of old furniture! This contract was 35 times larger than our turnover at the time and could have destroyed us. We forged a great partnership with a social enterprise called First Fruit, and with their help we grew rapidly, and re-use and recycling of old office furniture is now the norm. We employed and trained more than 850 marginalised people and diverted more than 47,000 tonnes of furniture from landfill. My proudest moment came in 2008 when GreenWorks received the Queen's Award for Enterprise (Sustainable Development).	Find partners to work with – don't try to do it all yourself! When the big chance comes along – grab it!
I regularly meet amazing people with great, imaginative business ideas designed to make the world a better place.	Sharing helps you reflect on what works and what does not.
Every day, our members employ people from difficult backgrounds to collect, repair and deliver furniture, electrical goods and other items to people in real need.	Working together proves that the whole is bigger than the sum of its parts.
I want to put my formula of shared experience, trust, hard work and enthusiasm to the test. Tree Shepherd will work with public authorities, businesses, social enterprises and local communities to create new, worthwhile jobs for the people who need them.	I will no doubt learn a lot of new lessons…

Bibliography

Books

This book draws on several truly inspirational and thought-provoking texts that seemed to be guiding me on a journey. Everything I read seemed to reinforce the convictions that were growing in me from personal experience working with people on the margins of our society. My writing can in no way compare to the style and panache of these books, but it springs from the same urge to set out in one place the things that I believe.

Giono, Jean, *The man who planted trees*, Random House, 2003
 Probably the most beautiful and inspirational book I have ever read.
Hutton, Will, *The State We're In*, Jonathan Cape, 1995
 Superb analysis of how we could do things better.
Mawson, Andrew, *The Social Entrepreneur, Making Communities Work*, Atlantic Books, 2008
 Great demonstration of how communities can thrive if they are given a chance.
Putnam, Robert D. and Feldstein, Lewis M., *Better Together, Restoring the American Community*, Simon & Schuster, 2003
 Superb analysis of how to build communities.

Schumacher, E. F., *Small is Beautiful – A study of economics as if people mattered*, Abacus, 1974

The ground-breaking description of how we could organise an economy that helps people; really comprehensive and well argued.

Wilkinson, Richard and Pickett, Kate, *The Spirit Level*, Penguin, 2009

Breathtaking assembly of data that powerfully demonstrates that fairness is beneficial to everyone.

Academic papers

As I started to write this book I wanted to know if the slice of life that I had witnessed was as representative as I thought. I rapidly realised that many people and organisations have spent huge amounts of time and resources amassing data and analysing the divisions in our society. If anything the situation seems worse than I had feared. I have themed the most important academic research papers and reports that I consulted in the section below.

For confirming my instincts about how bad the situation actually is

'Twenty-five years and three recessions, how much difference have they made to claimant rates in high-unemployment neighbourhoods?' (2010), Alex Fenton and Rebecca Tunstall, University of Cambridge and Centre for Analysis of Social Exclusion, Seminar Paper, London School of Economics

'What's going on in the Labour Market', a presentation by Professor Paul Gregg, University of Bath, for the Social Market Foundation, October 2011

Work, Worklessness and the Political Economy of Health, Clare Bambra, Professor of Public Health Policy, Wolfson Research Institute

for Health and Wellbeing, Durham University, Oxford University
Press, October 2011

Quarterly Statistical First Release, Department for Business Innovation and Skills, 29 March 2012

'Voluntary sector organisations working at the neighbourhood level in England: patterns by local area deprivation', David Clifford, Third Sector Research Council, August 2011

Back to the floor, BBC2 TV series

Wealth and Assets Survey, Office of National Statistics, 2006–8

For helping me to understand what went wrong

'Do schools make a difference', Harvey Goldstein, Professor of Social Statistics, from the Centre for Multilevel Modelling at the University of Bristol, BBC Radio 4 *Analysis*, 30 January 2012

'The New Deal for Communities Experience: a final assessment report', Elaine Batty, Christina Beatty, Mike Foden, Paul Lawless, Sarah Pearson and Ian Wilson, Centre for Regional, Economic and Social Research, Sheffield Hallam University, for the Department of Communities and Local Government, March 2010

'Evaluation of the Single Regeneration Budget: A Partnership for Regeneration', Final Evaluation Report, part 3, Rhodesi, Peter Tyler and Angela Brennan, Department of Land Economy, University of Cambridge for the Office of the Deputy Prime Minister, February 2007

For helping me to develop my ideas on how to tackle unemployment and poor education

Plugging the Leaks: Making the most of every pound that enters your economy, Bernie Ward and Julie Lewis, New Economics Foundation, September 2002

'Creating Shared Value', Michael E. Porter and Mark R. Kramer, *Harvard Business Review*, January 2011

Fightback Britain: a national report on the social enterprise sector, survey by SEUK, the national body representing social enterprises, 2011

'The Role of Attitudes and Behaviours in Explaining Socio-economic Differences in Attainment at Age 16', Haroon Chowdry, Claire Crawford and Alissa Goodman, Institute of Fiscal Studies, September 2010

'More Jobs Less Waste: Potential for job creation through higher rates of recycling in the UK and EU', Anna MacGillivray, URSUS Consulting, report commissioned by Friends of the Earth, September 2010

'Waste to Wealth: Recycling Means Business', Institute for Local Self Reliance, February 2002

'Local initiatives to help workless people find and keep paid work', Pamela Meadows, Joseph Rowntree Foundation, 26 June 2008

The Social Entrepreneur Revolution: Doing good by making money, making money by doing good, Martin Clark, Marshall Cavendish, 2009

For confirming what does not work

'Understanding Workless People and Communities: a literature review', Helen Ritchie, Jo Casebourne and Jo Rick, DWP Research Report 255, Institute for Employment Studies, June 2005

'Young people's education and labour market choices aged 16/17 to 18/19', Claire Crawford, Kathryn Duckworth, Anna Vignoles and Gill Wyness, Centre for Analysis of Youth Transitions, December 2011

The Influence of Parental Income on Children's Outcomes, Susan E. Mayer, Knowledge Management Group, Ministry of Social Development, New Zealand, 2002

For helping me to understand what did not happen

'Understanding the worklessness dynamics and characteristics of deprived areas', Helen Barnes, Elisabeth Garratt, David McLennan and Michael Noble, Social Disadvantage Centre, Oxford Institute of Social Policy, University of Oxford, for Department of Work and Pensions, 2011

'Immigration and social cohesion in the UK', Mary Hickman, Helen Crowley and Nick Mai, Joseph Rowntree Foundation Report, 20 July 2008

Acknowledgements

This book has been effectively 20 years in the making and I could not have completed it without the considerable assistance, encouragement and guidance of so many people.

Special thanks must go, first of all, to the innumerable people I have worked with over the last 20 years or so: the men and women whose stories fill this book, and the countless others who have worked with me at various times. All of them share a commitment to a better way of doing business and a more equitable world. It has been an incredible and deeply fulfilling journey and I have met so many amazing and generous people along the way. I would like to thank those clients who stuck their necks out to persuade their firms to buy from a social enterprise, the funders who came forward to sponsor me in the difficult start-up phases and the politicians who backed me.

I would especially like to thank the people who joined me at critical stages in each enterprise: George Broom, who financed the first van at Papercycle; George Cook, who engaged me at Cybercycle and who offered vital help in setting up GreenWorks; Ann Britton and Narinder Singh from Gateshead Council, whose unstinting support enabled Renew North East to take off; Scott Keiller, who persuaded Comet to get involved in the Renew project right from its outset; and finally, Peter Watherston from First Fruit, for his extraordinary boldness and long-term commitment in collaborating with GreenWorks and for his ongoing friendship. They all helped me on my journey and gave me inspiration and support at crucial times.

Next I would like to thank my fellow social entrepreneurs for providing a constant source of vision and energy. There are far too many to name.

I am grateful to Emma Price-Thomas for guiding my reading at pivotal moments, and to John and Ann Smalley for providing refuge in Northumberland while I shaped my earliest thoughts. Julia Heynat has been a constant source of help with her patient and dogged research into the inner recesses of the government's statistics. At Vertigo Communications, I would like to thank Jenny Boyce for her tremendous organisation and guidance and Catherine Best for her brilliant and incisive editing.

Above all, I want to thank my wonderful wife Sharon and my fabulous children Conor and Aoife for their patience and constant willingness to listen.